Life with Jake

A Father's Story

Kirby Wilkins

LIFE WITH JAKE
A Father's Story

Lychgate Press
Copyright © 2015 by Kirby Wilkins
First U. S. edition

Distributed by Partners West
Bellingham, Washington

ISBN 13: 978-0-9882887-7-5
ISBN 10: 0-9882887-7-X

Library of Congress Control Number: 2015936492

LYC█GATE

Corvallis, Oregon
editor@lychgatepress. com
www. lychgatepress. com

Book design by Rachel Harris
Cover design by W.L. Gilroy
Cover photos by Frank Cornejo
Front: *By the Walker River*
Back: *On Monitor Pass*

For Jake, father to the man

And for Jennifer, whose love for Jake sustains us

Contents

Life with Jake

Prologue

IMAGINE A MAN who didn't like most athletic contests because no matter the score, his team was going to lose or he was going to lose. For whom holidays masked family misery, and every cough was pneumonia or cancer. For whom weddings led to divorce and good intentions were self-aggrandizing. Whose candidate would lose and, if not, would be a severe disappointment. A pessimist, in short.

Imagine a man for whom the darkness of winter begins at Halloween with fright masks. They aren't funny to him. They remind him of real skulls moldering in Croatia, Iraq, Cambodia. So Halloween masks and skeletons begin his descent toward Thanksgiving when families bounce between dad, mom and whatever partners and step-siblings and grandparents have assembled—bloated, drinking too much, watching sports, waiting for Black Friday. Which is a concept he has no clear idea about, but finds an appropriate designation for the day after gluttony, guilt, obligation.

Now imagine such a man, fifty-five years old, approaching December 1, 1992, when the thirty-eight-year-old woman with whom he is living will give birth to a son. Because her age called for amniocentesis, they know what is coming. She had always wanted a child. She came from a large family and was generously endowed with such parental qualities as nurturing and unconditional love. He had never been interested in having a child because, some might say, he was too self-absorbed. His sister's children might have helped prepare him for fatherhood had he and his sister been close, but he knew his nephews mainly from photographs. To be honest, he was spooked by young children, those little Rorschach tests that would reveal your true inner nature. Kids and dogs. He could usually fake it with dogs, but kids took one look and rushed to mom or began to cry. Or at best looked forlorn. It was expected that you would be eager to pick up infants, that you would have the common sense to cradle their head as you bounced them, murmuring appreciative nonsense. For him it was easier not to hold them in the first place.

He could almost count the times he had performed such a pantomime, but now he was turning fifty-six, and his own child was about to be born at the darkest time of year. He was teaching English full-time at a community college, commuting several hours, and working on a third novel. He and the mother-to-be were living in the house he'd inherited from his mother, a house where he had lived for several years as a boy.

The pregnancy was normal, so far as he understood normal. Pregnant women had always seemed mysterious, long-suffering, and slightly weird. Even after attending Lamaze classes, all he really knew was that babies were born, improbably, from between the thighs of women. There then came a vague time involving diapers, dandling on knees, funny little clothes, squalling, then toddling around getting into things, more crying, grandparents, nursery school, kindergarten. Finally they appeared in his college classes writing stories of tortured lives and dysfunctional families, in the debris of which they often found a silver lining. He was not much inclined toward silver linings, since they negated the virtues of pessimism. But as a teacher, fair-minded to a fault, he celebrated turning points in addiction, adversity and loss.

So it's December 1, 1992, and despite the mandatory seasonal glitter and guilt-driven shopping, despite the repulsive piped cheer, he is not especially gloomy. He is too distracted. They arrive at the hospital with friends, birthing being very public these days, for an event that has occurred billions of times beyond his ken. Oh, he'd witnessed a friend's home birthing with midwife, which had gone well; but now here at the hospital, at the university where he expected the worst at football games, he is just one more man awaiting the birth of a first child (or what at his age might have been a grandchild).

And here is the odd thing. He is not the least bit pessimistic. He hasn't known enough to form a protective shell of pessimism. Like any other man, he simply awaits the miracle of humanity. The mother's water bursts in a dramatic geyser, startling them all, and he watches the nurse search for a fetal heartbeat. He is not alarmed because this is a famous hospital. Even as the nurse becomes increasingly frantic, he remains dumbly confident.

Finally, she says, "Could you push the emergency alarm?"

That would be the red button next to the bed where he is standing beside the woman who a year later would become his wife.

He pushes the red button.

Immediately a nurse appears, the sort you would want in any emergency, formidable, taking charge in a way suggesting that the attending nurse was still learning her trade at a teaching hospital. The obstetrician himself appears. Evidently, prior attendance is not required of a busy man who, now, must make an instant decision. Too late for caesarian. He exhorts the mother to push, and she does, bursting blood vessels in her face.

For a pessimist, whatever occurs is generally an improvement over the worst, and if the worst should happen, it is still possible to say: "See, I told you it was going to happen." But this time, he's run with the optimists and something is badly amiss. But what? In a hospital like this what could possibly go wrong with something as quotidian as birth?

Doctors and attendants surge into the room, seize the silent neonate, allowing no cuddle time for his dazed mother who won't see him until many hours later in the beeping and hushed confines of the Neonatal Intensive Care Unit. A wizened little being, unconscious, wired, tubed, and presumably as human as newborns in the viewing room, lies silent in a controlled environment where he cannot be touched. Beneath his clear plastic dome, he looks like something in an Egyptian museum. And now the father, unprotected by anticipatory pessimism, for whom the notion of paternity is alien, this man wants only one thing: for this being, his son, to stay alive in his incubator. He wants his team to win no matter the odds.

The Beginning

Unplugged (12/19/92)

On the eighteenth day,
the last catheter, heart monitor, IV is unplugged
and we take him home
to sleep in the big bed.
Rolled on his side
unable even to cry,
a little wrinkled but beautiful,
the baby named Jake.
Our son.

Presence (12/20/92)

Never before in my life
have I slept with a baby.
My clumsy body moves
in nightmarish half-sleep
while he lies between us,
dusted by lamp light,
like a moth.

Baby's First Bath with Daddy (2/4/93)

Head propped on Daddy's knees,
bald and chubby as Buddha,
fat legs floating free,
he faces a most peculiar creature –
all bony and hairy, angular.
Perhaps he's meditating on that other warm bath
sixty-six days ago
and how it ended.
His mother and I won't forget.
Neither will he, I expect,
if he learns to remember.
Meanwhile, I hold his fat feet,
and we drowse together in warm fluid.

Jake Smiles (2/11/93)

Like a sea anemone
an area around his tongue
crinkles out of shape,
and we are so delighted
that our own faces distort.
But here's the main thing:
that seeing us purse our lips,
and wave our tongues,
he knows we're out here,
that our wrinkling faces are for him.
That's the main thing.

Jake Cries (2/13/93)

This is not to be believed:
that such a rosebud mouth
in such a genial face
could explode.
Like some deep sea creature
brought to the surface.
Gaping at us.

Jake Discovers His Appendages (2/23/93)

Slurping at his fist,
chin slick with saliva,
he finds a finger.
Sucks on it.
Then a thumb.
The rest he'll save
for another day.

Mudras (2/24/93)

Yes, Hindu dancers –
that's where I've seen them before –
my son's hands raised in sleep
like the dancer's mudras
praising god.
The dance before knowledge,
the dance of first shapes,
when whatever it is
we can't remember
first appears from the void,
and we spend the rest of our lives
looking for it.

Hello Out There (2/25/93)

His mother says,
"Are you trying to talk, Jake?"
I look down at him on the bed.
"Hi," she says again and sure enough,
his mouth tries to imitate hers,
and there comes an odd sound.
The aliens want to communicate!
I open my mouth enunciating
the way you do with foreigners:
"Hi," I say.
The alien mouth opens.
A sound comes out: *Aiiieeee*.
So we're not alone in the universe.
And we're all smiling now.
Welcome to our home.
Aiiieeee.

Inconsolable (2/27/93)

I've never heard anything quite like it –
having never actually seen a mother
beside her dead child or a victim tortured –
this keening of the unbearable.
As his eyes roll back
tears streaming,
body rigid,
hands clenched,
and without language to explain,
his screams echo down the brainstem of our nightmares.
We can only do this one thing –
we can pick up our baby
and against the unendurable distortions of his body
press our own flesh.
This much we can do.

Picking Up Auntie at the Airport (2/28/93)

No, Mommy can't hold you,
not while we are driving.
That's the law, son.
You simply *must* tolerate this plastic bucket
called an infant car seat.
See, in the event of an accident,
these straps will prevent you
from being launched like a twelve-pound
cannon ball through the windshield.
Please, your screams are drowning us.
See how we search one another's stricken face
in the oncoming headlights.
Mommy and Daddy are strapped in too.
See, it's the law, son.
Please stop screaming. Please.
Your screams are tearing at our bodies.
Like the accident we are not going to have.
Yet. Please. It's the law.
Really.

Baby Butt Poem (3/1/93)

Sticking up in the air
is a naked baby butt
with the rest of him attached.
Whoever thought this up,
it strikes me as a fine concept.
So soft.
Pattable.
Hey, Buddy,
Bubba, Babu.
Hey, you,
Boo Boo.

Holding Babies (3/6/93)

It's become clear to me
why some people love to hold babies –
usually women, it is true,
but not always.
Now I understand
their desire to reach out
to cradle,
dandle,
rock.
Now I can even endure that moment
I had always feared –
when the baby,
like a Geiger counter,
scans your adult core
for warning:
babies and dogs always know.
Now I too know
why some people can hold
dangling happy babies
like bunches of grapes.

A Visit with God (3/14/93)

Instead of the nice Asian neurologist
who watched over him in NICU,
a large Caucasian resident appears
and begins to study his star charts –
those obscure constellations of our baby's brain.
Big as a defensive lineman,
he asks about our baby's back arching,
and his eyes not focusing.
We are evasive until the chief neurologist comes in
and looks at the same charts.
Has he had a vision test?
I think it would be a good idea.
And just like that we're back in NICU
crying for his tiny, damaged brain.
Only this time we don't dare cry
because God is speaking:
Come back in three months.
We listen humbly.
We do not say, "But, kind sir,
his pediatrician said problems,
if any, wouldn't show up for a year."
No, we keep our heads bowed.
We have learned not to ask too much of God.
We are grateful to do what we are told,
to carry our baby with the wandering eyes,
irregular EEG to the outer chambers
where a kind woman pricks his heel,
squeezes out a blood sample,
and his screams are pulled from us like intestines.
Beneath the harsh florescent light,
our lungs constrict,
our brains scatter,
and our own eyes rove wildly.

The Brave Mother (3/24/93)

A librarian by training,
she goes to the medical library
and returns with *Cerebral Palsy*,
a word I do not remember hearing from the doctors.
"Remember those early developmental signs?"
she says. "How he held up his head,
rolled over early, stood on stiff legs?"
How could I not remember such delights?
"Well, those were actually symptoms
of unnaturally high muscle tone."
So his rigid screaming in the car seat,
that's an angry rebellion of his body?
"Also," she says, "cerebral palsy can affect
cognitive function."
My brain freezes.
I look down.
His eyes are bright,
watching us.
Bright eyes.
Good.
Because our own eyes are dull and fearful.
"Also," she says, "there's another term we need to know."
My body goes rigid.
High Risk.

High Risk (3/25/93)

Sure, timber fallers
miners, steelworkers
far above city streets.
Sure, teenage drivers, smokers.
Actuarial tables, okay.
But not this.
Not our baby's bright wandering eyes.
Not his arching body and beautiful face.
Surely not these reaching hands.
These sounds.
Not this.

Boo Boo Makes It Through the Night (3/27/93)

His mother says,
He's so beautiful asleep.
And it's a simple truth this morning.
In the smooth, round face
his closed eyes are luminous as lamps,
and he breathes like the night's breeze
through our window.
Of course, standing here
with rank breath and matted hair,
we made it through, too.
From one side of the tipped earth
to this side of night.

Does He or Doesn't He? (3/28/93)

Mean *hi*
when he says *aiiee.*
His mother says:
"At four months it's
just the sound they make."
"But if he says *aiiee*
when I say *hi,*
what's the difference?" I say.
"Because," she says, "he hasn't
a clue that it means hello."
Aiiee see, I say.
She smiles.
I smile.
He smiles.

Taking Baby for a Walk at Full Moon (4/5/93)

Riding grumpily in his Snugli,
face to face with Dad,
we walk past shadowed lawns,
curtained windows,
night-blooming jasmine.
He's swinging from my neck
like the moon on its gravitational tether,
his face moving from shadow to moonlight.
Back and forth.
Light and shadow.
Finally, his eyes close.
Mine, dilated by night,
remain open.

Baby Legs (4/6/93)

There is this to say about baby legs –
that you do wonder how they will ever
get bony and hard, hairy.
Or how, down at the end,
such soft pads will ever develop
calluses.
Or what such small toes
could possibly hope to accomplish
beyond wiggling at your touch.
To hold the leg of a baby
is to forget
all you ever knew about legs.

Sleep Burglars (4/7/93)

His first night alone in the nursery
he wakes crying.
We listen in the next room.
Suddenly, as if garroted, he stops.
No sound. None.
Quickly we tiptoe over squeaky floors
into his room,
but under the blanket
there is movement in the night light.
We freeze – fearful but delighted –
two sleep burglars caught in the act.
Holding our breath.
Vanishing.

Doubles (4/17/93)

At last Jake's pediatrician drops her good cheer.
Yes, she says, *there will be some physical problems.*
It'll be clearer at six months.
But, doctor, I don't want clarity.
Don't dwell on it.
Think of the good things.
But, doctor, I am a pessimist.
At home, Mom breaks down sobbing.
I hold her tight, holding myself far tighter.
What else can we do but go on with our days?
So I play tennis as planned,
but I'm stumbling, watching balls pass with bare pretense.
We're getting slaughtered, me and my partner,
until he falls, clutching his ankle.
He felt something pop in his Achilles.
It's numb down there, he says.
Naturally, we help him to his feet,
and naturally he insists on limping off by himself.
Let us help, we call out. *We can carry you.*
He doesn't look back.
Later, she says, "How could you play tennis?"
I say, "I don't know."
I don't mention my stumbling body.
I don't even mention the torn Achilles.
I say all I can think to say –
"I don't know."

Sobbing (4/19/93)

At the sound of my sobbing,
Jake, who is expecting to play,
grows contemplative.
He's never heard this sound from his father.
How can I help, Dad?

First Time in the Pool (4/19/93)

Under an evening sky
on the San Francisco Peninsula
among orange and loquat trees,
and supported in my palm,
my son floats in the chlorinated water
of a friend's swimming pool.
A helpless bundle of toes and fingers
joined by everything in between.

Going Under (4/20/93)

It's like a bath isn't it –
whatever surrounds our living
and transmits it?
As water transmits the sounds
of small animals creeping the ocean floor,
or hovering in deep mythic shafts of light.
As in the next room,
at the very moment
Mom and Dad are doing it
(for the first time since his birth)
Jake wakes crying.
When we finish sheepishly, he stops.
Love and exclusion from it –
like the water surrounding us,
carrying our deepest clicks and squeaks.

Healing (4/24/93)

Incense and drums
because there's a Tibetan lama,
right here in Menlo Park,
in our living room,
near the famous hospital
where our son was born and nearly died,
and where cerebral palsy was diagnosed.
In topknot and robe and bare feet
the lama, a friend, has spent years in solitary retreat.
Now he's purging our son's karmic accretions,
first by water, then by fire.
And our son does quiver,
as if something were leaving his body.
Either that or he's having a mild seizure
to which he is prone.
Afterward, he smiles, is cheerful, vocal,
though restless in sleep.
And once again, I weep.

Looking Over San Quentin (5/15/93)

Her house overlooks death row.
This is our first day beyond the law
of doctors, therapists, and insurance,
which won't pay an alternative healer.
She's saying, "What insurance *will* pay for
is trying to break his damaged movement.
That's all wrong. Instead we'll let him lead the way.
We must go with him."
Her Israeli teacher,
the Feldenkrais master himself,
had a black belt in judo.
So I'm thinking this must be like judo for the brain.
We've been told she has extraordinary powers,
even refers to herself as a witch,
and he is relaxed and responsive in her hands.
She rolls him back and forth on a massage table,
his head anticipating each move.
"See," she says. "He's very intelligent."
"Basically, he's a healthy child."
He sleeps all the way home.
That's unusual we agree.
After our 100 mile round trip and $150,
we agree something did happen.
But is she healer or charlatan of hope?
That we don't ask.

Laugh Master (5/18/93)

Sometimes he sees me coming
and his entire face is transformed:
from a lifted lip of acknowledgment,
to a droll and crooked twinkle,
to a full-wattage smile.
And just that fast, my own face
becomes a twitching mess of wet clay
in the hands of a master.

Shaman (6/5/93)

Who would think that a hand,
resting palm down,
could bring such joy?
His babble and laughter, of course.
But a relaxed hand?
Please.
But like all great teachers
Jake lets us discover the obvious.

No (6/16/93)

Not another test
Not another measurement
Not another placement
Not another norm
Not another specialist
Not another surrender.
In the streets of Sarajevo,
the alleys of Mogadishu,
the fields of Chernobyl
and even here,
we must fight.
Even here.

Mr. Vestibular (10/5/93)

He's clasping his hands in glee and alarm,
mouth squealing wide,
as I swing him *way* up and *way* down –
the way Daddies do.
His doctor has a name for it: *vestibular motion.*
Could help balance and a wandering eye.
Even walking.
You never know.
So, between Mr. Vestibular and me,
there's plenty of glee.

Mr. Crooked Head (10/6/93)

At 4:00 a.m. I bring him crying to bed
where he begins slurping at Mom's sleepy breast
like an old man at his soup.
I wait as she drifts back to sleep.
He turns his head, eyes me, snorts,
a terrifying sound at this hour.
Quickly I stroke his back,
watch his eyes close,
face grow round and smooth,
body relax around a belly of warm milk.

Doubt Worm (10/7/93)

His mom tells me about
their last visit to the healer
who has given us such hope.
It seems she was working on his back,
twenty minutes into the hour,
when he turned on her with a sharp irritated cry.
She snapped back: "Guess he's done."
Mom said, "Maybe he just wants down."
And so he did, wriggling at their feet
like a worm. Our little doubt worm.
"And then?" I asked.
"Then we left."

Jake Goes to a Wedding (10/16/93)

In Carson City, Nevada,
the justice of the peace runs the marathon
and wears a hairpiece.
In a state once famous for divorce,
our friends, husband and wife of 30 years,
are witnessing our marriage.
That night at our cabin Jake won't stop screaming,
and we can't find the reason.
Must be the altitude, we decide.
It's good to have a reason.
Neither married couple gets much sleep.

Cathedral of the Universe (11/13/93)

Jake wakes at 1:00 a.m. and I go in,
stroke his head and back
as he thrashes in his crib,
screaming in rage and despair
that his mother must hear in the next room.
I stroke his back and smooth head,
in a way that I know must feel good.
Oh, how I wish my own back were so stroked,
and my knobby head.
Slowly he stills in the night light,
fists clenched beside his face.
I cover his sweaty body,
leave his head exposed, that dome,
the cathedral of the universe.
Which just fits my large hand.

Sweet Measure of Another Time (11/15/93)

Standing over his crib as he sleeps,
just before morning commute tears the day open,
I hear the train whistle two miles away.
My mother would have heard it, too,
before she died in this room.
He must hear it, too,
without knowing what that sound means.

Jake Delivers (11/16/93)

Here he comes,
back arched,
head tipped to look behind him,
kicking himself over the bed.
If, when every infant fiber says move,
and you couldn't crawl,
mightn't you try this way, too?
When his head reaches the edge,
he's delighted, but also alarmed,
and tries to sit up.
Since he can't do that either,
he gives one last kick over the edge
into Daddy's arms and another world:
shoes, odors, carpet, dust balls.
And he did it on his own!
He celebrates with such squealings
that I wonder was I ever so pleased.
As now, Jake?

Hey, Guys (11/18/93)

I'm pushing Jake through the neighborhood,
body rigid, eyes wandering,
when we pass some boys on roller blades.
They're carrying hockey sticks,
wearing knee pads and helmets,
and are very intent on business.
The last boy calls out:
Hey, guys, wait up.
I glance into the red stroller.
It's a chill November day,
and it all comes back to me.
All of it.

Small World (11/20/93)

Yet another healer overlooking San Francisco Bay.
She has a grand piano and shelves of music,
a portrait of herself with Yo Yo Ma,
and by way of introduction tells us about
an autistic child who began to play at her piano.
His parents said, "We aren't paying for music lessons."
Now they listen.
Her teacher was the Feldenkrais master above San Quentin
who, she says, has a genius for teaching.
And for making money, I think.
Of course I say nothing.
Because the world of healers is small,
and who knows what Jake may need.
The massage bench, where she works with Jake,
is beside a window where I see rain coming,
blurring the bay bridge, smudging whitecaps.
She is saying, *I wanted to be a concert pianist*
until I was injured.
Wind slams the window.
Branches thrash.
Jake startles rigid.
And I forget to ask how she was injured.

The Catch (11/22/93)

I'm on the floor watching Monday Night football
as Jake arches his way toward me across the bed.
On the screen, men in body armor
are trying to hurt one another,
or as we have learned to say:
Put a hurt on.
Make him pay.
Ring his bell.
They *sack, stuff and blindside.*
Sometimes, though it's punishable,
they *spear* and *leg whip.*
The odd thing is this:
I'm so engrossed
that I almost forget to catch Jake
as he plunges over the edge.
Hey, Pop! It's me.

Tooth (11/24/93)

In my new office as Chair of the English Division,
I hear alarming voices in the front office.
What? I call out. *What is it?*
The secretary shouts back, *Tooth.*
Jake's got a tooth.
I snatch up my phone.
Yes, his Mom is saying,
It's a big one, too.

The Charmer (11/27/93)

When we're out shopping.
He's couched in my left arm,
while I fill the grocery cart with my free hand.
Oh, how they turn and stare.
such a large old father,
carrying such a beautiful baby.
Mostly women, true, whose own children
toddle underfoot and straddle hips,
ride their carts like chariots.
They say, *Oh look at the baby.*
I dread the next question.
How old is he?
One year, I say.
Oh, he's so sweet, they say.
Yes, he is, I reply.
How sweet you will never know.

Trust Me (11/28/93)

"Now," the optometrist says to me,
"you put it in."
It is a long-wear contact lens,
stuck like mucus on the end of a stick.
I bend back his long lashes.
His trusting eyes stare up.
"You're too cautious," she says.
"Grasp the edge of the lids."
I stretch open his eyelids,
point the stick.
He doesn't blink or resist,
even when the lens touches down,
even when it pops inside out he doesn't cry.
"Not to worry," she says.
Next time I stick the lens to his cheek.
"You'll get the hang of it," she says.
"You're just afraid of making contact."
Next time he flinches and I give up.
Even his mother, who wears contacts, can't do it.
He cries all the way home.
We are silent.

Jake Practices Raspberries (12/1/93)

He gets it!
How to purse his lips and blow.
What a fun sound!
Not to mention what an amusing spray
of carrot moosh, milk, saliva.
Also quite therapeutic.
So says the occupational therapist.
Might even help him talk.
So as we celebrate his first birthday,
that terrible time of goodness,
he's spouting like a whale
migrating down our coast
toward another latitude
and the sweet calving ground.

Tongues (12/9/93)

Make him use it, the therapist said.
His tongue.
Have him eat graham crackers.
That seems dangerous to me,
but Mom says it's okay because
they'll melt right down.
I put a piece in his mouth,
leave an end sticking out,
like a tail for me to grab.
He mauls the cracker busily.
Suddenly the tail disappears
and I wait for gagging, choking,
my ill-remembered infant CPR.
He opens his mouth,
extends his tongue, grinning.
The cracker has vanished.
I extend another dry wafer toward his lips.
He accepts and closes his mouth.
Amazing! After all these years –
graham crackers.

Beating Dad (12/10/93)

He squeals and I imitate him.
He squeaks and I imitate him.
He shrieks and I imitate him.
We've got this thing going.
He gurgles, I try it.
He belts out a long wail,
I'm right with him.
Again.
Again.
My throat is getting sore, dry.
But he looks at me,
opens his mouth, waits, watching me.
Then his whole body goes rigid.
He screams, giving it all he's got.
You win, I say, breathless.
Enough. You win, Jake.
But Pop's got a lesson to learn.
He screams again.
Stop, you win.
He screams.
Jake.
But he's blowing the blues,
and I'm dumb before genius.

Relativity (12/14/93)

When I leave him sitting in his wind-up swing,
he cries immediately.
When I reappear, he stops.
I leave, he cries.
I reappear 20 feet away,
he stops.
It's quite apparent that some mysterious force,
sufficient to produce cries and tears,
is crossing the gap between us.
He smiles.
Really, Dad, it's so simple.

Falling into Happiness (12/15/93)

It's like Jake arching across the bed,
doing his version of the backstroke,
all legs, no arms.
How before he reaches the edge
and his head drops over,
he begins to laugh.
How I say, *What's going to happen, Jake?*
And then it does.
He falls.
I catch him.
Laughing.
Both of us.
How the whole way,
from his craned-back head
and upside-down eyes,
he knew where he was going,
and what would happen when he got there.
That he would fall into happiness.

Learning Curve (12/17/93)

Well used to bathwater now,
he's getting quite sophisticated.
As he studies his fingers
moving from one medium to the other,
I watch an idea form.
He bends forward,
dips his face.
I reach for him.
But he's blowing out!
Incredible! Blowing bubbles.
And how therapeutic!
I call to his Mom,
Look what he's doing!
She comes into the bathroom.
He does it again.
And we laugh together.
He doesn't get all the fuss,
until he forgets, breathes the wrong way,
gags, coughs
and then tries again.

Boo Boo and the Salad Bowl (12/18/93)

The salad bowl, filled with popcorn,
sits between me and Jake on the bed.
He's lying flat looking at the ceiling,
I'm sitting up watching TV.
I reach for more popcorn
but something's wrong.
The bowl's tipped away.
I don't understand what has happened
until I see fingers gripping the edge.
I've never seen him use his hands this way.
I call to his mom, but by the time she arrives,
the bowl has rocked upright in a mess of greasy popcorn.
Sheepishly, I scoop it off the bedspread into the bowl.
She leaves.
Fingers appear over the bowl's edge.
I hang on.

With Mommy and Daddy in Therapy (12/19/93)

The couples' therapist,
dressed with great sophistication,
is a striking woman,
with a highly intelligent face,
and watchful eyes.
She sits opposite the couch
where Dad and Mom,
now husband and wife,
sit side by side.
Slumped. Slovenly.
On the floor between lies Jake.
I can't look at my new wife.
Neither can I look at the therapist.
All I can do is look at Jake,
holding a clever wooden toy,
amazed that he can hold it.
She follows my eyes.
The therapist does.
Jake looks up.
He's happy.

Vocabulary Lesson (12/27/93)

Out beyond the winter tree,
a fuzzy glow hangs in a hazy sky.
Jake's in my arms and we're whirling.
Where's the moon, Jake?
He turns toward the light and smiles.
Moon, I shout and point.
He looks and laughs.
Moon, Jake.
And sure enough, as if we're on a carousel,
here it comes again, a gummy glow
tangled in tree branches and cold air.
I look down and read his expression:
I've got it, Dad. Moon. What could be simpler?

Under Construction (12/28/93)

Through redwood trees Buddha appears,
a huge statue nearing completion and ready for gilt.
Seen through trees, the enigmatic smile startles me.
A man is working on Buddha's foot.
A red baby stroller appears in front of Buddha.
It's pushed by a Tibetan lama.
Inside the stroller is my son.
Buddha, eyes lidded, smiles.

Vision at Last (12/29/93)

Three days before New Year
that crazy idea of contacts,
for a one-year-old with cerebral palsy,
becomes the reality of glasses.
So now he's Mr. Four Eyes, the little professor.
On the way home, the glasses bother him.
The sun is low, blinding at the year's nadir,
and he's screaming, clawing at the towel
intended to protect him.
I brake to avoid an accident.
Up front, we clamp our jaws.

World View (1/1/94)

Held in place by flexible wires
wrapped around his ears,
new glasses dominate his face.
His eyes look out.
Our eyes look in.
Between are the glasses.
His mother says, *You're so cute in glasses.*
Later she sobs.
I'm so used to rubbing his face against mine.
I hold his glasses to my eyes.
The right lens is clear, but the left makes me dizzy
as though I'm tottering on a cane.
I put them back on his face.
His nearsighted eye moves, focuses.
And there we are.

Well, Well (1/11/94)

In the bath,
Jake sticks his tongue into the water,
lapping like a dog.
Then he glances sidewise at me
with a strange new smile,
as if he knows something I don't.
Like it's some big deal
sitting in warm liquid
held in Dad's strong arm,
sticking your tongue
through the surface of the water.
Say, Dad, have you tried this?

Watching the Door (1/14/94)

He's stuffed with baby aspirin
when we come home from therapy.
He cried a lot, the sitter says.
He was looking at the door
the whole time you were gone.
And it's true,
the moment we came through the door,
at the moment of recognition,
he began sobbing.
So this is it, then?
How loss begins?
An open door at dusk.

Anger (1/23/94)

We're near the shopping center
walking Jake in his red stroller,
arguing the usual way,
when I explode: *Fuck it!*
and shove the baby carriage toward her,
turning away as I've done all my life.
As any child knows,
the whole point of turning away
is not to look back.
But, after a dozen angry steps,
I hear a voice.
And there, alone on the sidewalk,
is a red baby stroller.
She also turned away
but had looked back.
How long before we realized the horror?
Cars would have stopped.
Who picks up the baby?
What do they think?
What do they do?
What do we do?
Looking back,
having done such a thing.
Knowing it.

Emotional Absence (2/10/94)

Beneath the coffee house arbor
three men and a baby sit in cold rain.
Clear plastic covers the arbor,
drapes over the baby carriage.
One man says, "Our couples' therapist,
she gave her a new goddamn term.
Emotional absence. It's driving me crazy."
The manager of the coffee house says,
"You know, since we can't talk to women,
we ought to do this more often."
The third man, father of the baby, says,
"Well, at my college we offered men's issues classes,
but they were poorly attended."
Unusual in this part of California,
snow is falling on the surrounding hills.

48

Yeah, or the Origins of Language (2/23/94)

I'm daydreaming at breakfast
when I hear a sound like *yeah*.
Startled, I turn toward his baby chair.
Want more? I ask.
Again, he makes the sound.
I dip the baby spoon into the jar of baby goo.
He opens his mouth.
As I lean forward with the loaded spoon,
I'm watching his mouth.
He's leaning forward watching the spoon.
Yeah, I say.
He swallows.
I wait.
He opens his mouth.

Corrupting Influence of Peanut Butter (3/6/94)

Of all things, his pediatrician says *peanut butter*.
He's sure to gain weight on peanut butter.
So I buy a jar heavy with classrooms and camping trips,
gummy tables, torn white bread.
I think of dogs trying to swallow it.
This stuff could choke a baby.
So I daub his tongue.
Very cautious.
He blinks.
Considers.
Definitely weird but ... okay, Dad.
He opens his mouth again.
The real danger comes later that night
when Mr. Paunchy tiptoes into the kitchen,
smears thick slabs of bread.
This stuff could kill you.

Going to Safeway at Fifteen Months (3/7/94)

I'm racing the stroller through Safeway
because he could start screaming at any moment
and we come around a corner too fast
startling a man and woman about my age.
"Sorry," I say.
They smile graciously.
"Your son or grandson?"
"Son."
"He's beautiful."
"He is."
They go one way, we go the other.
When I look back they're watching us.
Embarrassed, they turn away.
I look down at Jake.
He doesn't care.
I shouldn't either.

Cooling Down (3/18/94)

Jake's lean body thrashes in his crib,
head whipping
butt pumping
arms flailing.
From time to time,
he raises his head as if astonished
to find himself strapped to this body.
I'm stroking his back.
My hand slows.
Please, I think, *please*, and lift my hand.
He jerks awake with a cry,
the way I jerk from a dream of falling.
I begin stroking his back again,
lightly so he won't know when I stop.
He doesn't.
I cover him.
And then we all sleep.

Riding in the Truck (3/20/94)

His car seat's in front of the pickup
facing backwards as the law requires.
Until he's twenty pounds.
What is it about trucks and Dads?
The ghost odors of firewood?
Musty sofas, mushroom compost,
rototillers, floor sanders, chainsaws.
Hard-earned dents and scrapes.
I remember getting into trucks
with building materials, guns, machinery,
trucks driven by men who could do things.
My dad never owned a truck.
Jake looks over at me with a wry smile.
Wind ruffles his hair and mine.
It's Sunday, going to the dump.

Accident (9/26/94)

All accidents are meaningful now.
Jake is swinging in the park,
tilting toward his right-eye patch
intended to strengthen his left eye.
As I let the swing go toward Mom,
an off-leash Dalmatian dashes toward us.
Jake's leg smashes the dog, spins the swing, and he screams.
Since he's afraid of dogs, this is a nightmare.
His mom and I look at his legs.
The dog's owner says, *His foot looks a little funny.*
I don't say it looks funny all the time.
Jake's quieting down.
He's okay.
We're all relieved.
Except for the dog.
It's back on leash.

Jake Listens (10/17/94)

Sitting in the tub,
balanced so well my single finger
on top of his head supports him.
"Feel how good that feels," I say.
I mean his balanced body.
And the way you can tell when people hear you,
when animals understand you,
when everything else falls away,
he listens.

Propping (1/7/95)

Leaning forward on propped arms
he's sitting by himself.
"Look at you sitting by yourself."
He looks up at me, pleased,
and pitches sideways on the bed.

Splish Splash (1/24/95)

I learned to say it from his book,
Splish, splash, in the bath.
Splish, I say, and his rigid arms flop.
Splash, I say, and he does it again.
Now he reaches for his plastic boat,
watches his hands obey.
These days he's reaching for door frames, cabinets, trees.
The world is out there.
There's so much to learn.
Eh, Pop?

Sink the Cup (1/25/95)

In his bath,
Jake reaches for the floating plastic cup,
sinks it.
I refloat the cup.
He sinks it again.
Then, as if he were holding the cup,
he brings both hands to his mouth.
See, Dad.

Rollers (2/1/95)

He's into rolling over.
Developmentally, it's a big deal.
His approach, however, is unorthodox:
hands bent backward,
pushing off his wrists,
arching his back
turning his head,
until he flops over.
He's very pleased with himself.
When he stalls sometimes, I can't help myself.
I give him a little push.

Psychodrama #23 (2/8/95)

You don't want to hear about disabilities, she says.
We're in the kitchen and it's true.
I've just put him to sleep and his door is open.
She's about to warm coffee,
but the microwave often wakes him.
I can't believe it.
She hits start.
He begins to cry.
I look at her.
When can you live your own life? she asks.
We're finding out.

Floating (6/4/95)

Jake's stretched on his back
as I tow him in circles around our friend's pool.
Gravity's all gone.
His legs are relaxed,
hands outstretched,
floating free as a dream.

Under the Bed (6/16/95)

More than anywhere else, he vocalizes under the bed
where he can reach up and touch wooden slats and futon.
Today's syllable is *Ma ma, ma ma*.
We smile and listen up on the bed,
imagining what it must be like down there,
Dad's huge foot on the carpet beside you,
to be making these sounds like speech.

The Lip (6/21/95)

At any sign of departure,
Jake's lower lip protrudes,
after which he howls with loss.
Only his mother can reassure him:
there is no such thing as loss.

Homes (8/28/95)

Taking Jake to pre-school for special needs kids
is like driving my mother to the convalescent home.
He's just as rigid and uncooperative as she was.
You'll have friends there, I say.
You'll socialize.
She didn't believe it and neither does he.
She managed to die at home,
but he has no choice.
He's going to day care.

Playing Ball Backwards (9/1/95)

He's lying on the bed,
and I'm rolling a ball toward him.
Not in the usual fashion,
so that he can see it coming,
but from behind his head.
He has to crane to see it coming.
Then, at just the right moment,
he whips his spastic arm backwards,
and the ball flies off the bed.
Laughing, we do it again and again.
His body is working perfectly.
Backwards.
It's our secret.

Four Years Later

IT'S THERAPY DAY. The physical therapist is young, just out of school, and has lived in Reno. So I'm talking about Reno back in the forties when I lived out of town in the sagebrush, before The Biggest Little City in the World became the ghastly sprawl where this young man grew up. My parents divorced when I was ten, his parents five years ago, my wife left a month ago.

"Plumb Lane?" he says. "That's your old road? It's four lanes and big houses now. There's big money out there."

For a moment I'm back on the gravel road to our house standing beside one of those forlorn phone poles that seemed to hum to me. I thought the sound came from voices squeezed through the wires. After my mother's death I found a crayon drawing she'd kept in a box: orange and red poles along a blue road with a stick figure pressing its head to one of the poles. My name was crudely printed on the road. Second grade I suppose, a bit older than my son learning to walk today.

He cannot talk. When excited, he squeals, when upset, he cries; he has a variety of soft sounds which accompany an open mouth, as if saying yes, and which mean yes. A scrunched-up face means no. A large variety of other facial expressions mean many things that grow ever more complex with passing years. But his smile takes no interpretation. His smile lights up rooms and draws smiling people from all over. He is one of those kids so beautiful that people turn to look at him. Of course, it's tricky these days whether they stare because of his beauty or because he sits oddly in the grocery cart, or because, at his age, he's still in the cart being pushed by Grandpa. Or is it Daddy? So many codgers are having kids these days with a second wife. Or third in my case.

The therapist from Reno sits on a wheeled stool behind my son who just weeks ago had surgery on his left hip. It was done in New Jersey, and now he's wearing a brace with rods fastened to his thighs, keeping his legs from crossing as he attempts to walk. The therapist holds him by his waist, exhorting him to stand tall, and he does, sort of, leaning forward as if into a strong wind. He bends a knee and swings forward a leg at the end of which is a foot encased in a kind of plastic boot that keeps his Achilles tendon stretched and his foot positioned. He plants that foot on the hardwood floor, swings his stiff arms forward while the young man sitting behind him on the wheeled stool helps shift his weight.

Surprisingly, my son must learn to shift his weight in order to free his opposing foot for the next step in order to move his body forward, a body weighing just thirty-nine pounds buck naked. One of the things I've learned is that ratio of weight to age is important in assessing human development. At six-and-a-half, my son just makes the cut.

As he swings another leg forward, I say, "Way to go, son, nice walking."

The therapist from Reno, hands on the boy, says, "Nice weight shifting."

Together we've invented a game to motivate his walking. The therapy center has a number of bolsters covered in bright vinyl for easy cleaning. Usually kids are stretched across them, but in this game I stand the bolsters on end, like crayon-colored phone poles, to lure him forward. As he approaches one, he raises his stiff arms and pushes it over. Then I move the bolster to the end of the line. Today, we're luring him toward an open door onto a patio, the longest walk we've attempted, and he's knocking down bolsters with gusto.

Finally, all that stands between him and the open door is the biggest bolster. It's bright red, taller than he is, and has given him problems in the past because it's so heavy. He stares at it, considering. Secured at the hips by the young man's hands, he leans forward, but instead of using his hands, he butts the bolster with his head, and the bolster, instead of going down, rocks back and butts him in the head. He studies the situation. Finally, he takes one more step and begins to punch awkwardly with his tight, bent arms, like a prizefighter training on a big bag, and the bolster goes down.

He screams a sound that everyone in the therapy center has come to associate with delight. He has transported his body to an object bigger than himself and has caused it to go down. He has acted on the world. The effort causes a thin thread of saliva to leak over his chin and wet his shirt.

Unlike the smaller bolsters, the big bolster does not roll when it hits the floor. It simply thumps down. Thump! Like a bag of dirt or a body striking the hardwood. The young man rests on his wheeled stool while I move the red bolster outside. My son seems drawn to the light, or perhaps to the threshold itself, and watching his body grow more alert with each step, I imagine that this act of moving from one environment to another by your own actions must be very exciting. For me, learning to walk has been a strange business. Learning to see. To feel. To imagine.

The therapist is not only young. He is strong and wiry, practices Kung Fu, and uses his back in a way an older therapist likely would not. He leans from the stool, supporting the boy's wavering body for amazingly long periods of time. Now, backing through the door, I feel sunlight on my back, see it strike my son's knees, and imagine him feeling this same summer warmth. A plane drones in the distance. Not a jet but the good old-fashioned sound from my childhood, a prop plane headed for the Reno airport. The tall red bolster has once again become a phone pole, and I've just learned that the humming wires overhead do not actually carry a voice, but a faint electrical pulse, a vibration of electrons which can be translated into speech.

Or a wild shriek of excitement.

He stands on the threshold, hair riffled by afternoon wind. His open mouth, his eyes, his saliva-slick chin—everything speaks of overpowering joy. As he yells into the sunlight, two hands rest lightly on his hips supporting him. Then, for a moment, the hands lift, and he stands before me.

My son Jake.

An Epic Ride

I BOUGHT THE TRICYCLE in a box. Assembled, it looks surprisingly like my own in a Reno photograph. I have no memory of riding that one on a gravel road, but I'm looking quite confident under a straw hat, Nevada sage in the background. This tricycle I've modified with a seat-back, chest-strap, foot-clips. Since steering is so difficult for him, and a sudden turn would flip trike and rider, I've locked the handlebars so that he can only ride straight ahead on his mission: to bump a motivational bolster with the front tire. When it falls, he screams with delight.

So far he's only ridden on the hardwood floors of the therapy center with two of us helping. This is our first ride alone, and what better place to practice than an elementary school at the end of summer? And what better school than my old elementary school? It was famously progressive in those days, encouraging us to find our own way rather than the right way. We studied at our own pace, followed our interests, and hit high school in the fifties in a peculiar state of mind. At least I did. Whatever was in was out for me. My idea of fun was reading *The Lonely Crowd*. Now I'm thinking that if Jake enters public school, he might come here, to his dad's alma mater, and close the circle.

I unload the trike and substitute a rolled air mattress for a bolster. Working alone, however, I have trouble securing him to the trike, making him so agitated that I can't step away to set up the air mattress. He's in his fear-posture, rigid body, mouth agape, arms arched to either side of a torso tipping to his left; for whatever neurological reason he always tips to the left. I hold his shoulders, massaging, feigning confidence. When he relaxes, I keep one hand on him and with the other hold out the bolster at arm's length. He stares at it from beneath his helmet.

Then I utter the magic words: "That bolster doesn't stand a chance, Jake."

He rocks back and forth, trying to remember which foot to push down, but before he can decide, the air mattress falls over. The school's breezeway is living up to its name, especially at this time of day when fog rushes inland over the Coast Range. I reposition the mattress, he rears on the pedals, tips to one side and I catch him. Next try is better, and he peddles into the air mattress, knocking it over, screaming with excitement and accomplishment. Now he's ready to ride a deserted elementary school, concrete block buildings, concrete walkways, covered exterior corridors, while his father recalls a two-story clapboard building with gracious high-ceilinged rooms, a wide porch, and steps leading down to an open field and a creek.

As Jake grows more confident, I can move the air mattress farther away, until I'm standing about where the tetherball pole would have stood, about where we played mumblety-peg with pocket knives. So I'm about fifty years distant when he launches his next bolster attack, backwards, toward an entirely unanticipated hazard: a deep gutter and sure smash-up. I reach him just as he figures out the problem and starts going forward, highly amused at the unusual sight of his running dad.

"You know, Jake," I say, suppressing my alarm, "the tetherball was there and I parked my bike right ... over ... there." I send an encouraging glance toward the long vanished schoolhouse, but he couldn't care less. He's now so eager to ride that I retire the air mattress under one arm. We start uphill.

"Where'd this hill come from? I don't remember a hill."

Who cares? After the wood floors of therapy, it's a hill.

"This may be too steep for you."

No way. He peddles furiously as I surreptitiously push.

It's near dusk. A teacher is turning out lights in a classroom and leaving with a friendly smile. Two girls appear, looking askance at this weird father with a weird rolled-up air mattress under his arm and a kid too old for a trike who is screaming with glee or alarm or whatever. And is that the dad or a lech? Finally, off they go, two girls, self-conscious and dressed in the appropriate cool manner of just-adolescent girls, and now the school really does seem empty. Except for the janitor who appears and reappears, apparently paying no attention. Given the status issues at a school like this, such as this school has become, he's probably learned to keep eyes averted when the Mercedes and BMWs and Land Rovers and Jaguars pull up.

At this time of year, the hot interior valleys of California suck cool air over the Coast Range, and the ensuing wind brings us the smell of wild land between here and the coast—bay laurel and tarweed. There should also be the smells and sounds of a creek with crawdads and frogs, but the creek has vanished, diverted through a culvert, I suppose, unless … I don't want to consider the alternative … unless I'm disoriented by the new buildings and have got it all wrong.

In the last open classroom, the janitor is working under florescent lights. The coastal fog bank is now pouring toward us like a tidal wave obliterating the hot day, and Jake's hands and face are cold to the touch, shirt wet with saliva. He looks chilled.

"We'd better head home," I say.

He protests. *Are you kidding? On a day like this? This is epic.*

It *is* epic, and he's eager to keep riding whatever direction his dad points him. Tonight we'll recall *Our First Epic Ride at Dad's Old School.* Naming is one of our games, and the expedition will be enshrined on a voice recorder used for sharing news at the Bridge School where speechless kids learn adaptive communication. The recorder looks like a small salad plate with a big red button on top.

He and most of his classmates can whack the salad plate to produce about thirty seconds of talk by a parent or aide.

My voice, a mélange of diction and perception I imagine for a boy pushing seven, will say: *Last week, I went for an epic ride with my dad. We went around and around his old elementary school. He told me lots of things from when he went there. It was a lot of fun.* Giving him voice pleases me.

Sooner or later even an epic ride must end, so I point his trike toward the parking lot. He's looking just the way a tricycle rider should look: upright, holding the handlebars, red-cheeked and smiling.

Once he's strapped into his seat, I start the car and the door locks click shut automatically. It's a security measure unnecessary for this particular child but a reminder that carjacking is in the news. In the rearview mirror, he's looking ruddy and runny-nosed, and soon, when he's sitting in one of my improvised chairs at home, we'll begin our collective memory of an *epic ride at Dad's old school that I may go to.*

The Parasites of Kings Mountain

LABOR DAY 1999 marks the end of summer vacation and the beginning of school, a cycle governing my life until last year when I retired from teaching. But this summer of separation has been no vacation as we move Jake back and forth between homes.

It's been grim schlepping him and his disabilities equipment between Mom's rental and the house where I lived with my mother after she left my father. What Jake thinks about all this we can only guess from his cries and rigidities. What *we* think is rarely spoken because, in our fourth month of separation, hostility reigns. My twenty-page letter trying to explain how we had come to this pass and proposing to keep us in one house while living separate lives was never acknowledged. Now, looking ahead to divorce, we divide Jake mathematically. And since Mondays are my day, I'm looking for something to do on this holiday.

"Hey, Jake, what if we go back to the Kings Mountain Art Faire?"

He gives me a big smile and wide-open mouth signaling an emphatic *yes*. Three years ago, the three of us went in the Honda, my bike on the rack, the Burley—his bike trailer—folded into the trunk. This time it's just the two of us in a cavernous van that follows Jake from parent to parent. At the summit, where Highway 84 to the coast crosses Highway 35 toward San Francisco, I pull over and glance at him in the rearview mirror.

"This is where I unloaded the bike and your mom drove ahead. Remember?"

He opens his mouth, but a bit cautiously. *Yes, Dad, I remember. But these recollections of yours can wear a fellow down.*

One of my obsessions in those days had been pulling Jake around the countryside behind my bicycle in the Burley. But I couldn't pull him up this mountain, so I'd brought bike and Burley to the summit, figuring to ride the last few miles to the fair. After his mom drove ahead, I realized my mistake. The busy highway was narrower and steeper than I remembered. Also I'd forgotten water. Also I'd left Jake's helmet at home.

It was before we had cell phones, so I couldn't reach her, though I see today it wouldn't have made a difference, because there's no signal up here anyway.

"Jake, do you remember riding up here? It was so damned hot, I almost died." And you with no helmet, and no water.

He opens his mouth. *What I remember is you complaining and swearing more than usual.*

I check the rearview to see what he's saying. When I look back at the highway, we're veering toward the center line. It's what cars had to do that day, swerving around a blue and yellow cart pulled by a wobbly and exhausted old man who was struggling to get around blind corners as fast as possible, and who, dangerously dehydrated, was nearly crying from exhaustion.

No doubt Jake has his own recollections that I can only guess at. *Sure I remember coming up here in the Burley, and how at the fair you stopped at the first beer booth.*

True. I'd locked the bike, detached the Burley with him in it, and pushed him to the first beer booth where, ignoring all advice on dehydration, I'd gulped five-dollars-worth of ice-cold draft beer. And since I figured Mom would drive us home, why not another beer? And since she hadn't witnessed the first beer and didn't know about the missing helmet, why not ride home, plunging down the mountain, Jake behind me shrieking with excitement as we made a game of staying ahead of Mom in the Honda—"She's way back, Jake, no, here she comes!"—causing him to laugh convulsively from anticipation and speed. A kind of hide and seek game on Kings Mountain.

This day we make a sober entrance to the fair. I'm pushing him in a collapsible wheelchair called an EZ Rider that looks like a stroller and makes him look infantile. People smile pleasantly at an old man taking such care to avoid tree roots, unaware that he and the boy are flying down the mountain and screaming with glee.

I suspect Jake, who has a good memory, is comparing trips in his own way: *Right, no Burley today. No sweat or swearing. But the same hamburger stand where we met Mom.*

True, I'm slathering goo from the same relish bar onto a desiccated burger, and, yes, we're stopping at approximately the same table where, instead of the Burley, I park the wheelchair and sit down. Instead of Mom, it's a wild-haired and hippy-looking young man who greets us. He stares at Jake very openly, watches me unpack Jake's juice and crackers, and I see that we've got a conversation on our hands.

Sure enough: "How's the boy?" he asks.

His opening gambit seems rude to me. Jake may be used to these questions, but I still have trouble.

"*The boy*," I say as sarcastically as possible, "has cerebral palsy."

"Have you tried Lecithin? Have you read *Alternative Medicine Magazine* about the power of oxygenated water?"

I look at him.

"Our environment is *so* degraded that it robs us of oxygen. Even though I live in Moss Beach where lots of well-oxygenated air blows in from the Pacific, I have two oxygenators."

Whether Jake is listening I'm not sure because the commotion of the fair has him standing in the footplates of the chair, straining against straps. It's the way his damaged nervous system responds to sensory overload. In my case, it's annoyance rather than brain damage tightening my body. Now the guy's in South America, where some disease is turning his stomach cancerous, and *they*, the doctors, want to cut on his stomach. Of course, I know about resisting *them* since *they'd* wanted to do major surgery on Jake's hips, and I had found an alternative surgical approach. But I'm not about to encourage him by admitting it.

"But, see, I cured myself. Do you know that environmental parasites cause 80% of disease? You can purge them with wormwood, which you can buy at Whole Foods in Palo Alto. You know domestic animals spread parasites when their poop turns to dust."

No doubt *poop* is for Jake's benefit, who seems to be ignoring him although you can't be sure. I've found that you can't talk over his head, as people tend to do around disabled kids, and I'm often surprised at what he hears in a crowded room.

"And the Chinese still use human waste. Do you know that Chinese parasites have been found in Penguins in Antarctica? That's how far they travel on the wind. I won't touch sushi anymore. I loved rare beef but won't touch it."

I still like sushi and rare beef, which is not a problem with this hamburger. A parasite wouldn't stand a chance. The relish bar, however, is another matter because the air is thick with dust, and dogs are crapping everywhere. You don't want to think about Chinese parasites and the relish bar.

"There's this electrical device," the guy says, "a zapper that purifies the body. I have two of them."

Zapper doesn't seem a very technical term, but I don't ask and he moves on: "This woman in Canada has a cure for cancer but it's suppressed by the Cancer Industry. Also, if you want to know more about parasites, look up Hulda Clark's book *The Cure for All Diseases*. For your son's benefit."

This last phrase, like a trap door, drops me into our nightmarish years of searching for alternatives: Feldenkrais, myofascial release, acupressure, electrical stimulation, cranial sacral work, conductive education, sensory stimulation, and sage baths. We even looked into hyperbaric oxygen chambers, compression suits, and patterning. Never a zapper.

I'm as tight as Jake straining against his straps, and we both need to escape. I jerk to my feet, abandoning burger and drink, but this guy's been stood up on before, and he's ready with his peroration:

"You'll have your boy up and on his feet in less than two years if you get a zapper and get rid of the parasites. Look at me."

I release the brakes on the wheelchair and push Jake away from the table into clouds of excremental dust. He's happy to be moving and begins to laugh, causing people to smile at us both. We pass beer and bratwurst stalls that, just looking at them, you know are full of parasites. Parasitic dogs strain toward us on leashes. Sunlight slants through the dusty air, and the highway, plugged with pedestrians, looks like a giant intestine.

The parasites of memory are breeding. How much raw sushi in my lifetime? How many shits in Delhi and in the Hindukush and Kashmir? How many rare steaks? And what about Sierra streams infested with Giardia? Had that blown in from China?

"Remember riding down the mountain last time, how I said, 'she's coming, she's getting closer,' and you laughed so hard I almost had to pull over?"

Jake opens his mouth wide in an emphatic and full-wattage *yes.* *Who could forget racing down a mountain with you and me laughing and Mom trying to catch us . . .*

"That was some trip."

Better than this one. That guy was so boring.

Our ride hadn't been *that* dangerous. I'd kept our speed down, and she'd protected our rear. That's the nice thing about memory—mine at least—it's malleable as wet clay. Keep working it and soon an irresponsible, half-drunk and helmet-less rush down the mountain becomes a special moment joining two Labor Days.

Like two segments of a tapeworm.

"That parasite guy was nuts," I say.

Jake doesn't look the least surprised.

What I remember about tapeworms is that each segment, if separated, will reproduce independently. Pretty soon, you've got worms everyplace.

"Nutty as a fruitcake," I say.

But Jake is no longer listening.

At the Sad Café

THE VAN RAMPS ARE DOWN when I pull into the Bridge School parking lot, and wheelchairs and students are being loaded by parents and aides. Jake's still in the classroom where his teacher and an aide are putting away augmentative communication equipment: switches, binders of glossy icons, and devices hooked to computers. There are no desks because the center of the room is left open to accommodate wheelchairs. That's where Jake is now, grinning, happy to see me, laser still strapped to his forehead.

"Sorry I'm a bit late," I say.

The teacher smiles. She's used to it and to me leaving his wheelchair behind when I carry him to the car. I remove the laser, like a third eye secured to his head by a stretchy band, unstrap him from the chair, and stand him up. Reaching around his waist, I tip him under one arm and head for the door. The teacher, surprisingly, comes with us. Outside she says, quietly, "Jake said he was sad today."

I translate this to mean that he pointed the laser beam at a sad icon on his Delta Talker. He has good head control, no small matter with cerebral palsy, and can move the red laser over an electronic keyboard. If he stops for several seconds at the icon with down turned lips, a soulless mechanical voice will say *I feel sad.*

"Any idea why?" I ask.

"No, I just thought I'd mention it."

Since she's talking to both father and son, I figure a message is being delivered to our split-up family. She knows the pressures of disability and is trying to help. Jake himself is laughing because he likes being carried under my arm, and I'm pleased that, at my age, I can still carry a forty-three-pound boy this way.

I look down but his face bears no resemblance to the droopy, down-turned lips of the sad icon. "I'll talk to him," I say.

She returns to the classroom, leaving the word behind like an explosive device. I enunciate it carefully: "S–a–d."

Jake looks up.

Perhaps at the end of a school day he was only tired and, pressed to say something about feelings, chose the icon with down-turned lips as the closest thing to tired. Except *tired* is a yawn and raised arms. He could have chosen that. What if, with all the fall color, he was only *melancholy*? Or *blue*? *Doleful*? Not, I hope, *depressed* because it's such a fad these days—so many kids and parents taking medication. How about *downcast* or *dejected*?

I look at him under my arm, but he's grinning. Nope, not *dejected*. What about *angst*? A favorite of mine until he was born.

"Maybe you meant *angst*."

He isn't listening. Instead, tipped on his side, he's watching kids spill from the public school next door. Happy, giddy kids. At their age, third grade I'd guess, I'd have been shuffling out of class beside the Truckee River looking somber, even though the divorce I didn't know was coming was still a year away. Actually, some of these kids do look a bit somber. There's likely more divorce here than in Reno in 1946, then the divorce capital of the universe.

"How about *somber*, Jake?"

He knows I'm not serious, which is too bad because somber seems a good word. As a boy I had been somber with my father, more good-natured with my mother, neither of whom would have dared talk about feelings. Jake's mom certainly can and did in marriage therapy. Not me. I buttoned up. Perhaps it's generational. Feelings are in, stoicism is out, and I'm caught in some nether region between the two. I mean, okay, feelings are important, but do we have to talk about them?

Now, loading Jake into his car seat, I feel pensive. Choice is such a tricky business with him. Given a choice—*Do you want milk?*—he'll open his mouth for *yes* or grimace for *no*. At other times—*Want to go shopping?*—he'll say whatever you want to hear as a way to avoid conflict. It's a technique that I know well, sometimes attributed to the children of alcoholics.

Now I feel like a carnival barker selling sad. You looking for *sad*, little buddy, come on into the Sad Café. We got *hopeless*. We got *lonely*, *doleful*. We have *melancholy* with a side of *despair*. You want *miserable* or *desolate* we got it. And if you're feeling happy, champ, don't worry because happy folks, lots of bounce and smiley faces, can go straight to terminal *despair*. In fact, we guarantee *sad* or your money back.

The automatic gate opens, and we start up roads more suited to country than wealthy suburbs. Money buys rustic. At the first stop sign I open his favorite after-school treat, salt and vinegar potato chips, and reach one toward the back seat. He opens his mouth. When he closes it, fragments fall into his lap. At the stop signs ahead, he expects to get more chips, but I'm so busy practicing my sales pitch, I forget.

Son, are you sad or glad that we're going home alone? Your smile suggests the latter, but how do you really feel deep in your core being? Are you perhaps covering up being sad that your mother left? It's okay to be sad, Jake. You just need to talk about it. That's what everyone says. Get it out in the open. Feelings need to be talked about.

Looking in the rearview mirror I translate his expression: *reproach*. Of course! I've missed two chip stops. As penance, I decide to give him make-up chips while driving. It's a no-no, but the frontage road beside the freeway is empty, he's well forward in his car seat, and I have long arms.

"Are you still sad?" In the rearview, his expressive face is non-committal, no doubt working the angles, which I translate: *Since now you're giving me chips while driving, I'll want more, and then you'll have to explain, again, why it's not safe. And frankly that's pretty depressing. You want to talk about sad, let's talk about you.*

True, I'm stuffing chips into my own mouth and working my own angles. At the last stop before the freeway, I turn all the way to the back seat. Chips are scattered on his lap, the carpet, and stuck to his face. I give him two more.

"Last chance, Jake, are you sad?"

He scrunches his face. *No.* And only now, as my body relaxes, do I realize how much I dreaded the affirmative. Ahead is Interstate 280 south of San Francisco. Below and to the right is a white-capped reservoir lying in the San Andreas earthquake fault and filled with Sierra snow melt. Above are forested mountains of the watershed, protected and still wild. Fog, shaped by wind, streams over the mountains. Sometimes it comes like a tsunami, other times in a slow caressing of individual trees. A tsunami today.

"Look at the fog bank, Jake, it's amazing this afternoon."

I don't expect a response, and don't get one. Views are not his thing. What he likes are big trucks and buses. When we're passing one at seventy, his body twists toward it in neurological surprise and amazement. Once we're past, he relaxes. I check the rearview.

He's looking thoughtful.

I'd say that makes two of us.

The Night of the Living Dead

IT BEGINS WITH A PHONE CALL to Jake's mom for no reason except that, now that I have a cell phone, I can do it while driving. A new thrill. I'm still teaching fiction writing at the college, and I'm driving home late. There's no answer, which surprises me since, at eight-thirty, it's past Jake's bedtime. Over the next twenty miles I redial. Nothing. Then, something I've never done since she left, I stop by her small rental cottage, unannounced. It's dark, windows uncurtained. That's odd because she's very careful since a near rape in Berkeley years ago. My flashlight reveals Jake's favorite puzzle scattered on the floor. His special seat is at the table, his bags from school on the couch. It looks as though they just stepped out.

At home, I can't find a number for anyone who might know her whereabouts. I dial information, surprised that, these days, her closest friend has a listed number. A recording says she will receive no calls from blocked numbers. I have to think awhile to understand what that means. I'm the one being blocked. It's an accusation triggering my annoyance with the hyper-security that people subscribe to these days: gated communities, shredders, surveillance cameras, unlisted numbers. The recording explains how to unblock my number.

Her friend says that her own calls during the day have not been returned, and that's quite unusual. She'll call mutual friends. When she calls back, the news is worse: "She didn't show up at work."

"But they came home from school, his stuff's there."

"Unless," she says, "it's still there from yesterday."

Now the adrenalin is really flowing. "I'll call school."

But I have no contact numbers after school. Information provides a familiar name that turns out to be his teacher's sister-in-law, who gives me the number of his groggy teacher. It's getting late.

"Yes, Jake was at school. His mom stayed all day. It's the first time she's done that."

Which explains her absence from work. Obviously she'd gone home, dropped off his school gear, and left without responding to the messages from her friend who now agrees with me that an overnight is unlikely. She hasn't taken Jake anywhere overnight in their four months at the cottage.

I leave a message with the landlord asking to be let in to look for evidence of her whereabouts. I call mutual friends in Santa Cruz who, awakened, are alarmed but know nothing. Now I'm thinking of the Polly Klaas abduction and a recent rash of carjackings and rapes. Unable to sleep, I remember what my next door neighbor, a family therapist, had once said about Jake: that, being beautiful and speechless, he was a prime candidate for abuse.

At first light, sixteen hours after they would have returned home from school, I begin calling and alarm is spreading among school staff, parents, friends. I return to her cottage that looks more vulnerable than ever. Our beautiful child, the perfect candidate for abuse, has been kidnapped, is being tormented. Or worse.

The landlord refuses to let me in. The friend arrives, looks through the window, and agrees she'd never leave things this way. I call the police. Nothing. We call local hospitals, standing side by side. I call parents from a preschool for disabled children that Jake attended several years ago. I reach people I've never met. One mentions a memorial service for a child. I call that number rehearsing what I'll say: "I'm sorry for your loss, but by the way, have you seen my ex-wife and child." It turns out not to be the number of the bereaved family, and the woman who answers is shocked to hear about the memorial—a merciful death some might say, for a child suffering not only cerebral palsy but multiple sclerosis. She gives me another number.

A woman answers. When I identify myself as Jake's dad, she says cheerfully, "Oh, you must be looking for Mom."

She comes on the line, laughing. "How did you know I was here? No one knew where I was. I arranged this visit weeks ago."

I'm so stunned by her laughter that I can only stammer my fears. I pass my phone to her friend, who, not amused, says, "It did look serious."

I am so grateful for those words. I have tears of relief and gratitude in my eyes, but I feel the way a zombie looks, completely without feeling. Dead. She passes me back the phone, and I can barely say goodbye. The friend and I go our separate ways. Now I must call a list of alarmed people, explaining how every lead had pointed the same way—unreturned calls, not showing up at work, uncovered windows—but all is well.

I'm still on the phone when she pulls into the driveway and comes into the house without Jake. She apologizes for something that's not her fault, and I try to explain, without being too accusatory, how deep my terror had been, deeper than anything I remember.

"Maybe I'll get a cell phone," she says. "To avoid this sort of misunderstanding."

Since it's Jake's night with me, I carry him into the house, smiling and happy, put him in his seat at the kitchen table. She watches cautiously from a safe distance, as if ready to flee. On the table is the list of people so difficult to assemble from this shredded life of ours. Even the family therapist, who thought our son a prime candidate for abuse, may never know about the night of terror next door—a case study of family dysfunction.

"I learned something profound from this," I say.

Her response seems hostile: "And what's that?"

My words are hesitant and come from a part of my being I've

never visited. "I couldn't go on living without him."

She turns away as if I've slapped her, and I realize, too late, that all my concern has been for Jake. I hear her car start. Jake's happy at the table, but I'm still a zombie. The imagined death and mutilation and sexual abuse and torment of this beautiful boy had come from inside me, some composite of twentieth century horror and all the centuries before that when rape, massacre, torture, killing of parents in front of children and vice versa were commonplace acts, even for the great civilizer, Alexander the Great. I can't watch violent films or even ludicrous horror flicks because those pictures, once allowed into my skull-bone-theater, will play and replay. And now this laughing boy has played there, even though I have censored the worst images, a luxury victims don't have—evading evisceration, hot irons, breaking bones, driven nails, the fetus cut from the armless mother, the impaled children, the sodomy. Victims can't change channels.

Even the death of my mother, in vivid color, was seen through averted eyes. In her death throes, all I could say was, *It's ok Mother, it's ok.* Not *I love you, Mother,* because in our family the L-word might have embarrassed her. Even while dying.

I touch Jake's head and say, "Hey, Doodlebug, good to see you."

Something in my voice causes a quizzical look.

I'd given everything I had but was helpless. And that, I now realize, is why I've kept myself so far from love. That it's taken sixty-three years to learn such a rudimentary fact is inexplicable.

But now I'm doomed.

The Two-Step, Up-Step, Side-Step, Down-Step

THERE'S A CORNER of the therapy center with a big mat and mirror along one wall. Jake's on the mat with his physical therapist, and I'm watching in the mirror thinking about dogs and cats. If they can't see another dog or cat in the mirror, what *do* they see? Jake himself shows little interest in his own image, but I'm seeing huge therapy balls, adjustable benches, plastic toys so obviously designed to avoid legal action that it's no wonder kids need so many of them. I see lots of shiny plastic surfaces, easy to clean, and with Jake drooling when he's excited, that makes a lot of sense.

The therapist and Jake are playing with a toy that will launch multi-colored and multi-sized plastic donuts from a peg. We hope this toy will motivate new movement, as bolsters did his walking and riding. The launcher sits on a platform requiring a step up. My job is to prepare the launch site by pushing donuts over a peg and locking them down against a spring. Then the therapist will help Jake, who, post hip surgery, is wearing a brace around his waist with articulated rods strapped to each leg.

With help, he can raise his foot, encased in a plastic orthotic inserted into an oversized tennis shoe. Stepping up, he is exhorted to straighten his leg against his own weight. Then, together, they raise the other foot and side-step to the launcher that I've cocked, ready to fire.

I watch Jake turn toward the launcher—twisting his torso is good for him—and reach for the trigger with a stiff arm and hand that is turned backwards. He closes his eyes, wincing at what is about to occur, and then the back of his hand touches the trigger and, POP, disks fly onto the mat. He opens his eyes and laughs hysterically.

His next task is to step down which, I think, should be a mirror image of stepping up, but the therapist says stepping down is more difficult and requires a more complex coordination of his body in order to bend one leg and reach the other foot down. I'd never considered that. It certainly requires a lot of encouragement as the two of them move slowly, formally—in the mirror and on the mat—down-step, side-step, front-step. I feel as though I'm watching two sons, the older helping his younger sibling find the rhythm of the dance, guiding his hips and helping shift his weight—*Way to go, Jake, now let's pick up the rockets.*

That means crouching, not easy in an orthopedic brace, and touching each of the rocket donuts (fingers if possible) as a signal for me to pick it up for reload. Watching their choreographed movements reminds me of square dancing in 7th grade, to scratchy fiddle music on a portable phonograph. It was the boxy kind schools used in those days where a steel needle rode a wavy record that bounced like the dance itself. But I could never have expressed joy then the way Jake does now. I was too self-conscious.

The mirror couple is moving together with Jake and his physical therapist, while an older man watches himself watching in the mirror. One of the nice things about square dancing was the way ages mingled and provided a rare occasion to be close to, to touch, older people. I'd danced with my best friend's parents and sister in schools and auditoriums all over the county. I had gone to live with them when my mother went to teach in Half Moon Bay, taking my younger sister to her fate. While I was square dancing or camping in the Sierra and Death Valley, she was attracting bad boys. One of them, a twenty-five-year-old Coastguardsman, threatened our mother with a knife when he took off for San Francisco with my sixteen-year-old sister, and later he nearly kicked the life from their unborn child. Our mother never forgave her. By that time I was studying math and physics at Reed College in Portland, Oregon.

This new dance, I decide, is the perfect time to use the video camera I bring and rarely get around to using. I raise the viewfinder to one eye, closing the other. In black and white, two dancers appear on the mat, two more in the mirror, and a man holding a video camera like a fiddle. I press the record button. When I stop recording and open both eyes, we all reappear in living color.

Nice, I say, zooming on Jake, *nice stepping, son. Nice side step. Now a back step. Now forward.* Pretty soon even the therapy balls and swings and scooters and wheelchairs are whirling to my fiddle. Jake is screaming, and I'm thinking bandanas and jeans, full denim skirts and checked shirts, tennis shoes squeaking on the gym floor as I swing from the moist hand of my surrogate sister to the dry touch of her mother. Now lock elbows and spin your partner. Can you feel it? How centripetal force is keeping us together?

Until, like my sister in Half Moon Bay, we let go.

Nice stepping, son. Way to go, Jake.

Swing your partner and do-si-do.

The Backpacking Story

CALL IT A FETISH: fifty years backpacking the Sierra, first in tennis shoes with heavy cooking gear, crappy sleeping bag, no tent and a pack repaired with wire or a sewing awl. Then the explosion of stuff—mummy bags, self-supporting tents, Polar Fleece and fantastic new packs with waist straps. Packs were the one constant, always at hand and ready to go. When travel luggage turned into packs with internal frames I was ecstatic. Now it's wheels. Everybody's wheeling about airports, kids wheel their packs to school, even car seats have wheels. Meanwhile my beloved old backpacks and luggage sit in attics or sheds, too beaten up to be given away. Because these days stuff has to be new: new technology, new design, new desires.

And for me, too, it's new packs, not to carry gear but to carry Jake on day hikes. First the Pony, then the Stallion, and now the Explorer with a multitude of pockets, straps, and god knows how much Velcro. What can be done these days with Velcro, nylon and a little aluminum tubing is amazing. Like the Burley I'd pulled behind my bike or his foldable wheelchair that I still use.

Photos show Jake in the pack of the moment looking, at best, contemplative, more often alarmed from flopping around town or on local trails. I, however, am looking pleased with myself in photographs taken by a companion. Having somebody along was a good idea since Jake couldn't hang on or balance and often needed rearranging. A case could be made that my backpack fetish helped dissolve the marriage. She didn't much care for all that jolly family-on-the-trail, sweating together through snakes and poison oak and low branches sort of thing. But that's behind us.

Today friends and their wives are helping. We're standing at the Pleasant Valley trailhead waiting for road dust to settle. It's a strange, hot fall, and since global warming has become a concern, such a dry year in the Sierra has resonance. We stand, dazed by the brilliance, staring up a valley where sluggish bends of the stream glitter like glass. Aspens are bare. Grass is brown. No snow is visible up high. It's near Thanksgiving, near my birthday and Jake's—63 and 7 respectively—and this is our first, and though I don't know it yet, last hike in these mountains before he's too big for me to carry. Or I'm too old to carry him. Whichever comes first.

And here's a strange fact. While I had wanted help from Jake's mother, I won't accept help from my friends. In their presence, I revert to mountain man independence.

"No, I'm ok," I say. "I've loaded him up lots of times. It's easier."

Which is true, sort of. It is easier for me to drop him into the pack, although he's pretty rigid from excitement and, perhaps, recollection of some of our walks with Mom leading to low grade hostilities followed by solitary trips lurching around city streets. Now, hoisting the unstable pack onto the tailgate, I *could* use help, but it's too late. I'm committed to competence. I slip my arms through the straps and stand with a grunt, reaching back for his feet dangling beneath the pack. Getting them into stirrups requires a lot of fussing because he's wriggling with excitement. Finally, one of the women can't stand it any longer, and begins to arrange his hands and feet. Someone else suggests stuffing articles of clothing to keep him upright. Sweaters and shirts appear and are rolled. They stuff the pack while I stand like a pack animal. Secretly, I'm glad of the attention. And I know Jake is. I can feel his smile.

Finally, we're ready for that special moment of a backpack trip, the first step under load. Since Jake's birth, the mechanics of walking are much on my mind: the amazing transfer of intent—through nerves, muscles, tendons, joints, skeleton—into a step forward, and then the next, seeking a rhythm that would carry a sixty-pound pack (a bit less today) over miles of rough trail and thousands of feet of altitude into the high blue days of the Sierra crest. Hard to believe, I wore no hat in those days, as if ultraviolet and cancer hadn't been invented. I came home thin and burned dark.

No question about hats these days. We're all in our sixties and retired. These couples have remained married to the end of the millennium, and they've grown to appreciate each other more, as some couples do in their later years. There's a deep sense of companionship as we start up the trail alongside the stream. They lead, I follow with Jake rocking back and forth and laughing at my first cautious steps. He nudges with his knees or kicks with his stirruped feet, as if on horseback, and, pleased by my rider's enthusiasm, I lengthen my stride to a clumsy half trot. Our collective weight, about two-hundred-seventy pounds I'd say, including pack and rolled sweaters, lands heavily on one boot and then the next. It's a jarring, clumping movement that makes him shriek with glee and wriggle, making it harder for me to maintain my balance.

No responsible father, much less one my age, would lumber over uneven ground with an already brain-damaged boy jouncing on his back. The others turn to watch us coming, and I can read their judgment. They are delighted by Jake's laughter but worried about consequences. He's laughing so hard he has trouble breathing, and though the November air is cool, I'm already sweating. They wait in the shade of a pine forest for us to arrive, and when we do, I take care to stand very erect and suppress my labored breathing.

We're not going far today, but already my mind is drifting into high granite country that Jake will never see unless he can be managed on pack animals. That seems more wish than possibility. Now swaying to his movement, I look at the stream below the trail. A fish is holding steady in the current, gills opening and closing.

Someone says, "Look at the size of that one." Fingers point.

Jake rarely responds to pointing fingers, so I crane my neck for a backward glimpse to see if he's looking. Nope, he's got his head back, staring up at the trees. Now both women are tending to him, adjusting his feet and head, wiping excited drool with a towel. Between them they have six grown children and three grandchildren and their touch carries so much experience that I feel like their child. As if they are murmuring to me, wiping my lips. Meanwhile, the guys are looking out over red willows at the dry valley and mountains beyond.

Jake begins to throw his body back and forth, goading for another run, and my body, like the big fish holding steady in the current, moves in counterpoint.

"Do you want to turn back?" one of the women asks.

"Let's go a bit further," I say.

Once again they move ahead while I linger on the river bank. A breeze riffles the water. The fish disappears. A floating cottonwood leaf lifts from the surface like a bright sail and begins to move upstream.

Jake wants to move and I know I'm going to do it again, stupid as it is, begin that lumbering half jog that so delights him. As we start out, he's rocking side to side with excitement, waiting for something even better to happen next.

I'm studying the trail with a practiced eye. A misstep now would be ugly. Up ahead, I see the others looking back to appraise this latest madness. But I've found my rhythm. I'm back in the high-country—sweating, body working the way it always did—as I pass them, dust spitting from under my boots, Jake screaming for more. Their voices fall behind.

Then I stop.

"Want some help," one of the men says coming up behind me.

"No, I'm fine."

His wife approaches. After a discreet silence, she says, "It's getting late, let's turn back."

I hate the idea of turning back, but she's right. She and the others seem hesitant to turn away and leave us, but I wait until they do. They glance back the way adults do with children, to see if they are following. I'm not. I'm still sucking air and gathering myself for the thumping strides that will make Jake laugh as if he's being tickled. When we finally clump out of the forest into open sunlight, he's almost hysterical.

Then I stop. Because there's no choice. At this altitude, my lowland heart is surging in desperation, like a fish on the line. Jake is nudging me forward. *More, Dad, more.*

But I hunch over, hands on knees, sobbing for breath and throwing him forward. I can feel his breath against my neck, fingers in my hair, and his alarm as he stops laughing.

"Are you okay?" someone asks.

"Sure. Just a breather."

After a long, awkward silence, I stand and head for the van. While I get him unloaded and safely on the ground, they watch.

No one offers help.

With the Partisans

SOMETIMES IT'S NOT a single moment but a sequence of moments that shapes life with Jake. In this case it starts with my capitulation: I just can't pull him in the Burley any longer. He's too heavy and I'm six years weaker, so I've decided to give up the Burley, and since the bike I pulled him with is a piece of shit, I've decided to buy a new bike. But my old bike shop has closed, so now, garrulously, I'm explaining my situation to the new bike guys.

"I just can't pull him anymore," I say, as if this reason to buy myself a bike is necessary to explain. But it's a difficult confession, and my tone must have struck them. Although they haven't met Jake, they listen with sympathy and seem more interested in his disability than selling me a bike.

"You know," the owner says, "there's a bike show next week in Las Vegas. We could look for something for your son."

Weeks later, I remember about Vegas and go back. Drawers are rummaged, a brochure appears showing a three-wheel bike intended for people who want to haul groceries around a trailer park. A young man is leaning back in his Joyrider, legs stretched in front of him, looking very cool and not the least disabled. How many brochures, crumpled phone numbers, and catalogs have led to nothing? But one day I call Florida, and a woman answers the phone. She does not put me on hold or transfer me to another extension. Instead she listens to my situation in the way that some people do, the way the bike guys did, drawing me out.

"We don't have many distributors on the west coast," she says, "but there's a dealer in Redding who modifies our bikes for disabled people. He's really into disabilities."

Sure enough, his voice from Redding says, "I love to get people out and about in ways that aren't ugly. I'm sure we can modify a Joyrider for your son."

But Redding, five hours north by Interstate, means an overnight which is a bit daunting. Who can help? A family trip seems ill-advised with divorce pending, but my friend Joe says: "Let's make it an outing. Just the guys. We'll eat pizza and drink martinis."

So late December 1999 finds us driving north up through the great central valley of California. With the millennium looming, there are signs and omens everywhere. It's strangely warm. No rain. No tule fog. No snow. Butterflies are emerging from cocoons months early. Before the Interstate, I'd passed through on my way to Reed College, followed a few months later by my mother driving my sister to a small California town for an illegal abortion. At fifteen she'd been raped on the beach. Joe came this way for poetry readings in Portland and to see his true love. Now those dreary valley towns have been bypassed, and we're traveling in a time capsule through bare fields adorned with blue herons and egrets. I sit in back holding Jake's hand, pointing out trucks and birds and talking about what a wonderful bike he'll get for Christmas. He's unimpressed. As far as he's concerned, his current trike is fine, and for him giving up the Burley was no big deal. It got us out of the house, and we both liked that, but the Burley was more my enthusiasm than his. The trike may be getting too hard for me to lean over and steer, but that's not his problem.

Up front, Joe's talking about his ankle healing from one of those moments when life veers at a quiet little stream in the high country on a summer day. Break my ankle and I can't get Jake to bed, into the car, to the table, to the toilet, onto his trike, to school, dressed. I think about such veerings a lot, and I'm feeling one happening now, not a broken ankle or strangling at birth, but another kind of veering. Like the surgeon in New Jersey who saved Jake's hips, or the therapist who pitched his wheelchair pommel over her shoulder to dramatize her own annoyance with such seating, or the young man from Reno who got him moving on foot and trike. And now a man in Redding, who thinks disabled people need to travel in style, is one more partisan passing us through enemy territory.

Jake drowses as we drift through teaching days (Joe's still teaching but thinking retirement), Joe's poetry and my attempts at poems and stories about Jake. It's nothing but old guys rummaging through the years and of no interest to a seven-year-old. Herons and egrets stand in the dry rice fields on either side of the Interstate, and hawks line the fences like spectators.

"Look at the hawks, Jake. See, those silos are for storing grain. That's Mt. Lassen. And see way up there, like a cloud, that's Mt. Shasta." Volcanoes are fine, but eighteen-wheelers are better.

We turn onto the old highway past empty lots and car rentals and whatever's left of Redding since the Interstate rearranged America. Even driving the van slowly, searching for our destination in the strip-mall chaos outside town, we miss it and have to ask directions at a small market run by East Indians and filled with video games and booze. The proprietor points across the street, his mellifluous English reminding me of India forty years ago.

His finger is pointing at a sad equipment rental shop that we'd already passed once. Inside the dreary shop is the man whose voice has given me such hope. He shows us a video of a quadriplegic pedaling with his hands. He points to pictures on the walls of disabled people riding his bikes. "I can't stand most equipment for the disabled," he says. "It's too clunky and ugly, designed to keep them dependent, but they're just like us." He looks at Jake in his wheelchair like a baby stroller.

"They want to get out and about in sleek contemporary designs."

Listening to him, I can feel what's been gathering all day sweep over me, a blind pulse of energy and enthusiasm driving me into obsession: Burley, backpacks, trike, modes of walking, sitting, communicating. Now this.

"I can modify anything you can think of," the man says, "car seats, standing supports, steering. See that photo. He's a logger crippled by a tree. He wouldn't leave his house until I got him on one of these classy bikes. Now he rides everywhere.""

I stand Jake from his wheelchair named after the 1969 movie *Easy Rider*. Once seated on the new red bike, he leans back, legs stretched to the pedals in front of him, and I see Peter Fonda on his chopper. That does it! I begin ordering everything the proprietor can think of: roll bar, steering restraint, upholstered seat, chest strap, foot clips, coaster brakes, wire basket, mirrors for the handlebars, and a safety flag to be flown on a wand behind the seat. When there is nothing more to order, I suggest taking the bike home tomorrow, Christmas Eve.

"These modifications will take some time, " the proprietor says. Of course they will. How stupid of me. "I'll ship it in January," he says.

Jake, who's been measured and pummeled for the past hour, is more than ready for a motel overnight with the guys, a promise of far more interest than a surrogate chopper. He eats spaghetti and sourdough bread from the ice chest, drinks Guava Berry Vita Boost and plays with his puzzles, while the old guys drink much-anticipated martinis, eat takeout ribs from Styrofoam boxes, and maunder through shared decades of friendship and common endeavor. TV is not watched. Jake sleeps on his futon beside my bed, and in the morning has his first motel shower in a fiberglass cubicle, a slippery business with a hung-over father, but more entertaining than a rundown equipment rental shop and a scary new bike. What's wrong with his tricycle? Just because it looks like something for a three-year-old, so what?

Much subdued by hangover, sinus, liver and ankle, Joe and I drive south into a low and blinding sun. Blackbirds swirl over the fields, and formations of migrating geese are now headed our way.

Jake slumps in his car seat covered with debris: goldfish crackers, graham crackers, salt and vinegar potato chips. Tomorrow, Christmas day, he will stay with Mom while I, avoiding any thought of the Christ Child, will ride my own new bike and imagine my son on his new chopper with mirrors, a jaunty flag, and padded seat.

Fourteen years later, the impractical coaster brakes and steering adaptation are gone; the bucket seat has been replaced by a seat from a wheelchair. The mirrors are gone. So is the flag. The wire basket has been replaced by a foldable carry-all, toe clips by wheelchair footplates, and people no longer say, *Neat bike where did you get it? Did you make it?* Kids no longer say *cool bike!*

Steering his bike like Peter Fonda on his chopper never worked out. I raise the handlebars to waist height, one of the features that attracted me to the bike in the first place, and walk beside him steering, while he (feet strapped to the pedals, torso strapped to the seat back) peddles to our favorite cafés and stores along our favorite avenues. We ride coastal trails and mountain roads on camping trips. We ride the Golden Gate Bridge. He's ridden thousands of miles, and I've walked as many.

Thanks to partisans passing us from one safe house to the next, my son has escaped again and taken his father with him.

Driving into the Millennium

WE STOP AT A PARK where you can look over the Gold Rush town of Jackson and be reminded of miners and boardwalks, whores and saloons, Chinese laborers tunneling through the mountains, and the new Walmart that obliterates such nostalgia. We're sitting at a picnic table familiar over the years, my arm around Jake's shoulders holding him steady as I feed him French fries. We've just had our first drive-thru fast food experience, and he'd been amused hearing me converse with a disembodied Burger King voice. But once here at the park, he spat his first Whopper bite onto the concrete table. So I've inherited his Whopper while he eats, with little enthusiasm, the fries.

Grinding uphill past us are pickups and SUVs with snow tires and lots of horsepower, locals I imagine, whose drivers glance at two picnickers on a winter-dead lawn: a solitary father and son eating lunch. Perhaps they notice something odd about the boy's posture, see the homemade seat he's in and finally get it. A couple of years ago his mom and I sat at this table eating homemade sandwiches and feeding baby food to a five-year-old: sweet-potato-and-chicken moosh from a jar. Now I'm dipping fries into a puddle of catsup and stuffing Whopper into my own mouth. The table's a wreck, scraps of lettuce, tomato, onion, pickle fragments, napkins, catsup packets, fries, Jake's milk and juice containers from his lunch box. He's leaning his head on my shoulder, or so it would seem to drivers. But I know that low muscle-tone in his torso makes him sag sometimes, when he's tired.

It's New Year's Eve of the new millennium, and we're going to meet Joe whose cabin is next to ours. It would be difficult getting Jake across the gulley to Joe's place, so we'll sit by our stove burning firewood a co-owner and neurologist, recently dead of brain cancer, helped split and stack. There are photos of him and his wife, drunk and happy, dancing at the cabin. Since there's no TV, we won't see the apocalypse moving toward us, time zone by time zone. We'll be asleep.

Back in the van, we head up Highway 88 toward Carson Pass and our first views of the pastel mountains and cloud shadows of the Great Basin, from which, in the back seat of a '41 Ford, my sister and I departed Reno headed for Stockton in 1946. Did my mother know then, crossing Donner Pass, that she would divorce the driver a year later?

How many trips to the cabin does Jake remember? Photos show him riding a sled or stretched in front of the wood stove with our friends piled around him like a slumber party. Photos show him riding his trike through the pines, me bent over steering. Photos show ten-month-old Jake at the Justice of the Peace in nearby Carson City where Mom and Dad were married. Their honeymoon dinner at a Virginia City casino has not been preserved.

When Jake is shown those old photos and asked if he remembers, his response is usually an enigmatic smile and an open mouth signifying *yes*. In some photos, his mother looks unhappy. In retrospect, she often was, at least when compared to courtship photos radiant with youth and passion and promise. Not so much youth in my case as vigor. However, photos of her next door at Joe's cabin after Jake was born show an animated, happy woman. Amazing how photographs can shape our present. Perhaps they are shaping Jake's thoughts on this trip.

At 6,000 feet I notice an odor—powerful and unmistakable— signifying a very loose stool. And from experience, I know there will be lots of it.

"Do I smell something?"

Jake laughs.

"Do I?"

In the rearview mirror, I watch his response: *Oh, yes, you do.*

"Had we better stop and change?"

Oh, yes, we should.

In this apocalyptically dry winter there is only patchy snow at this altitude, and I look for a dry spot to spread a towel.

"It's pretty slushy out there. Where are we going to change?"

That is for you, omniscient one, to decide.

A side road appears, familiar from our marriage trip. We'd stopped because ten-month-old Jake had thrown up organic baby food from our lunch stop in Jackson—a brilliant orange gush of sweet potato and chicken. After cleaning him up, we went on to marriage in a slightly acrid car.

I turn onto the slushy road and find a patch of damp asphalt. The odor is overwhelming—definitely a loose, sour stool, forecasting a major clean up.

I spread the striped beach towel on the asphalt road, set out diapers and wipes and two plastic bags, one for the diaper and one for his trousers which have revealed that dread phenomenon—diaper leakage. Which also means shit on the car seat. So that will need to be covered with another towel. On my hands and knees, I squeegee his sludgy butt exceeding even my pessimism—there's shit everywhere—finally snug up the clean diaper, pull up clean sweat pants. The car seat isn't bad, a small towel does the trick, and as I get him buckled in, I'm feeling well-pleased with my competence after seven years of practice.

I would have been less smug had I known that the van's starter motor had precisely five starts remaining. In a parallel universe, I'd have been stranded with a soiled diaper and a boy who couldn't walk, flagging cars for a tow truck back to a 150-year-old Gold Rush town that was boarded up for the millennium. But the car does start, and cheered by our few minutes in the forest, I put on the one CD we both like, *Canticles of Ecstasy*, twelfth-century liturgical music by Hildegard, the abbess of Rupertsberg, who considered her songs a celestial revelation.

We descend toward Silver Lake where ice is forming. In nine hours, calendars will flip to a new millennium. Survivalists are holed up with supplies and guns. Even sensible people are hoarding cash and supplies, as we discovered stopping for bottled water. I was standing in line with Jake in his EZ Rider wheelchair, when the woman behind us said, "Preparing for the end are you?"

I looked back. Rubber boots, wool shirt, and the weathered face of a local who knew a few things about survival.

"We have no water at our cabin." It was a simple statement of fact, but I sounded defensive.

She didn't respond, just looked at us, like … sure, I know you're fleeing town: *Cabin. Crippled kid. Water. Millennium. It takes all kinds.* But that was an hour ago. Now women's voices are soaring toward god, and we're passing trees and sun-warmed boulders swelling from snow banks. I glance in the rearview to see Jake staring out the window at the same boulders. He's got one foot propped on the seat in front of him, amused by something he's thinking about.

"What's so funny?" I ask.

He laughs in response. Laughter is a way for him to speak, and now, accompanied by *Canticles of Ecstasy*, we're goading one another to hysteria.

Leap Day

THE PHYSICAL THERAPIST AND I are looking at Jake on his new bike, ready to ramble down the highways of life. It's leap day of the new millennium, a difficult concept for Jake who loves calendars with a savant's capacity to know dates well into the past or future. I tried to explain leap year, how otherwise the sun and calendar would drift apart, but his knowledge of the calendar runs deeper than my explanation and he wasn't interested.

Last year at this time, we returned from New Jersey and the innovative surgeon who saved Jake's hips. Then we barely knew this young therapist, new to his trade. Now he's seen Jake through post-surgery, through assisted-walking with special orthotics, through trike-riding and graduation to a real bike. Without him Jake wouldn't be on this bike.

I tell him, "We're riding everywhere the wheelchair can go, and where it can't, like trails. The roll bar makes it easy to get in and out of the van and looks cool."

My effusions about Jake are usually contagious, but today he's not smiling. "Can we talk?" he says, gesturing for me to move where Jake can't hear us. Then he says in a voice that makes me lean forward, "I'm quitting."

The words don't make sense at first. We've become friends, closer since I began reading his novel about our shared landscape of Nevada and our shared background of absent fathers. "Jake's mom leaving you has made me rethink my own life."

We scarcely knew one another when she left and I'm startled by his confession. "Why?"

"The work isn't rewarding," he explains, "except for a couple of kids. Especially *him*." He glances at the boy stretched out on his new bike as if ready to ride into the bouncy spring clouds. Daffodils are up, acacias in bloom. It's that time of year in the Bay Area when spring comes a month early.

"Because of the bureaucracy?" I ask, heart constricted.

"No, they've been good to me. I like the people here."

Our voices are guarded in a way that could catch a child's interest, but Jake seems to be absorbed by traffic in front of the center. He loves cars.

"I just want to write," the young man says.

It's the book I've been encouraging, about the anguish of two brothers with an absent father in this postmodern era. Absence is the theme. Of father and family. The book arcs through sex, alcohol, drugs, and love for a brother whose mind is fracturing. The book is more frank than I've dared think much less write about my own parents. In fiction writing classes when I mentioned the unhappy childhoods of so many writers, I asked: "Does anyone here have a happy family?" A few timid hands would go up. Not many. "I'm sorry," I would say. It was a good laugh line.

But the anger in this young man, the potential mental illness of his brother, hints of suicide, the black despair have entered my blood and drawn us closer. We've shared hip surgery, faith in Jake's prospects as a walker and bike rider, and shared Jake's joyful response to a surrogate brother. For the past fourteen months there has been a magic circle around Jake and this young man and me.

"I'll stop by your house this evening," he says. "After I see my father."

In the past, he's combined visits to his father and to me, his writing mentor and surrogate father who has been searching for his own surrogates all these years. He sits with Jake and me at the table eating ice cream and strawberries. In Jake's presence, we can't talk about his impending departure, so we talk about his novel of a splintered family, how my notes about a previous draft meant so much.

"It made me believe in my writing," he says. And then, after a pause, "I need you."

He means as a writing mentor, but with Jake present and absence in the air, the phrase is electrifying. I want to say, *I need you, too*, but I'm mute. I don't want to burden him with undeserved guilt at leaving. But something else is holding me back. Never, to my knowledge, have I used the phrase, *I need you*. To need is to be vulnerable, to need is to expect loss, to need is to be pathetic and helpless. To need is to be abandoned.

But have humans come to this? That at ice cream over a table, they cannot express love to one another except through shared love for the boy being abandoned. And through fiction? After Jake goes to bed, perhaps unaware of the pending change, we continue talking in the kitchen.

"I don't want to lose our relationship," he says. "Or with Jake."

Other helpers, primarily women, have come and gone. The Filipina woman who had been so close to Jake had stopped by recently; the Brazilian sends cards; so does the Basque woman. The woman from Budapest is occasionally seen in the market, but has her own divorce to cope with and two children. The Russian called from Moscow. Helpers all over the world have remained tied by increasingly tenuous threads to this boy. *Remember that boy with cerebral palsy. What was his name? Jake. Who could forget. The Jakester. Jaker Shaker. The Jakemeister. El Bamboozle. Whose smile I can still remember in that unhappy family.*

What does Jake know? Surely he feels trembling in the strands supporting him over the abyss. Across the table sits a young man who loves him, whose hands, whether through martial arts or suffering, have such sensitivity in therapy; whose novel spans a single day but a lifetime of loss and betrayal. In the most recent draft, the one we talked about this evening, images from the

Inquisition and Hiroshima have appeared. From the Inquisition to Hiroshima: the modern American family.

Before leaving, he goes into Jake's room and looks down at the sleeping head sticking out of the comforter. That look, that look … as I've looked so many times at the sleeping head, suspended by so many strands spun by parents, teachers, therapists and caregivers all over the world. We, surrogate father and son, look down, yearning to be held by those same strands.

And the boy sleeps.

And this therapist will cease seeing him officially in six weeks.

And whether that has become clear to Jake or not, his web is trembling in the room where my mother died, in the house where I thought exclusively bad thoughts about my own father. The Inquisition and Hiroshima are interesting historical facts. Yes, faith can lead to ingenious cruelty and torture beyond the capacity of any other animal. Yes, a pure mathematical understanding of the universe can incinerate a city. But his novel has a long way to go, he's a beginning writer still needing discipline. I've worked with hundreds of such writers over the years. Some go on, some don't.

I want to embrace him, but to do so would open a world of loss. We both want to embrace. But we don't. Love leads to loss. That's enough for this leap night.

Blue

I'M PUSHING JAKE'S EZ RIDER wheelchair toward the stable when a woman strides past leading a very large horse with powerful haunches. I'm impressed by the haunches, both of the horse and the woman in riding breeches. How many years does it take to move with such authority among these animals? We enter the gloom and fecund smells of the stable where another woman tells us that our instructor isn't here but will arrive soon. "She'll be driving a Bronco."

We wait near a large arena where more women are doing impressive things with horses—commanding various gaits, a word I've learned from gait studies for the disabled. Jake doesn't really qualify since his walking is a communal effort guided by a therapist on a stool, while these women, erect as marine officers, command definite gaits from their animals, kicking their ribs, whacking them with riding crops.

A red Bronco pulls up crunching gravel and a woman gets out wearing threadbare riding breeches and accompanied by a girl a little older than Jake. From our phone conversations, I know this is her daughter who also has cerebral palsy. She's holding a riding helmet to lend Jake and shuffles toward us in a kind of controlled stumble, knees leaning together for stability. She has a gait. She hands me the helmet and her mother hands me a clipboard with an agreement I'm to read and sign, absolving the stables of liability. As I read, I can see there is plenty of liability to be absolved of:

No riding horse is a completely safe horse. Horses are 5 to 15 times larger, 20 to 40 times more powerful, and 3 to 4 times faster than a human. If a rider falls from horse to ground it will generally be at a distance of from 3.5 to 5.5 feet and the impact may result in injury to the rider. Horseback riding is the only sport where one much smaller, weaker predator animal (human) tries to impose its will on, and become one unit of movement with, another much larger, stronger prey animal with a mind of its own (horse) and each has a limited understanding of the other. If a horse is frightened or provoked it may divert from its training and act according to its natural survival instincts which may include, but are not limited to: Stopping short; Changing directions or speed at will; Shifting its weight; Bucking, Rearing, Kicking, Biting, or Running from danger.

So Jake is about to become a predator.

"The gentle old horse I told you about has gone blind," the woman says. "So Jake will ride a pony named Blue."

She looks at Jake's feet. "Does he have any shoes?"

I look at his feet. He's wearing sandals that flash red and blue lights. I say, as if expecting the question, "Sure." Fortunately, he does have shoes in the car.

"You might want to consider riding boots."

I try to imagine Jake's orthotics inside riding boots and say nothing.

"Do *you* have any shoes," she asks looking at my white athletic socks in sandals.

"No."

"Well, getting stepped on, even by a pony, can be uncomfortable."

She disappears in the region of large unpredictable horses, while I pull Jake's oversize shoes over his foot orthotics. I'm trying to adjust the girl's helmet on his head when her mother appears leading a pale golden pony that looks more horse than pony to me, and I think we've made a mistake. On the other hand, this woman has worked with disabled kids, including her daughter, and must know what she's doing. We're introduced to a young woman who helps her, a girl with no apparent haunches who seems a bit delicate. I wonder if she is strong enough for this? Am I?

"Well, let's get him in the saddle."

This is directed at me. Chagrined by my sandals and wanting to appear competent, I stand Jake from his wheelchair and, to the surprise of us both, swing him into the saddle. Since his feet don't reach the stirrups, I hold him up, while the girl on the other side keeps him from falling that way.

"Let's go then."

Jake begins to rock back and forth, hamstrings stretched by the saddle. Stretching hamstrings is good, as I've learned over the years. With the woman leading and two of us holding Jake upright, we enter a small arena plowed by hooves, and almost instantly my white socks turn brown. I know because I'm looking down a good deal at Blue's hooves. Jake performs a shriek from his repertoire of shrieks, but his face is full of light, so it's a shriek of delight.

"Not so loud," the woman says, "you'll scare the horses."

Blue appears placid, although on close inspection, she does seem to be rolling an eye in an effort to see what is happening on her back. She has probably never heard a screech quite like this. Any number of humans in crowded stores and classrooms had not. I remonstrate about screeching. He appears to listen.

"You don't need to hold him so hard," she says to me.

I'm inclined to disagree. On the other hand, things are going well enough that I momentarily lighten my death grip. Immediately I can feel Jake's body take over, correcting for each jolt. It's clear that his body is responding to the horse. Not just any horse. Blue. He is exhorted to feel Blue's shedding neck and does reach out a clenched hand. For a moment he even looks like a rider, albeit not one holding the reins or with feet in the stirrups.

We leave the arena for a trail, and as we start uphill, he is exhorted to lean forward, to make it easier on Blue, so I tilt him forward. He screeches again. At the top we stop and look down at all the activity around the barn and arena. Overhead are cheerful spring clouds. As we descend, he is directed to lean back and I oblige. We both know, now, that it's easier for Blue. When we reach more or less flat ground, the instructor explains that her daughter loves to trot.

"Do you want to trot, Jake?"

I'm not sure what a horse's trot entails, and I'm quite sure Jake doesn't know, but we find out simultaneously when Blue begins some kind of hopping movement. Jake begins bouncing, daylight showing under his butt, and his smile vanishes. But he does not cry, as I expect. Rather he seems to be concentrating, trying to figure out what on earth has happened on an otherwise pleasant ride. A trot, at least a pony's trot, is like riding a jackhammer.

We stop for trot evaluation. Jake expresses no firm opinion about trotting. I have an opinion but, before I can object, Blue starts trotting again, and Jake's expression shifts. It's difficult to get a read since I'm busy studying rough ground ahead of my trotting sandals and shit brown socks. I make a quick scan of his face: Terror? Nope. Pre-hysteric? Nope. Prelude to the fear/startle stance? Nope. It's some kind of inward concentration, like a constipated bowel. Which may not be far from the case, given the beating his butt is taking. On his other side, the girl seems quite oblivious and cheerful.

When Jake begins to sag over the pommel, we stop. "That's enough for today," the instructor says and looks at me as though I'll know what that means. I fetch the wheelchair, reach up and swing him down onto wobbly legs. He's looking a bit stunned. We schedule our next ride and I agree to buy him a helmet and boots at the tack shop.

She leads Blue to the stable while I push Jake's EZ Rider wheelchair toward the restaurant and tack shop. There's no wheelchair ramp, so I drag him backwards up steps and through a door into the strong smell of leather. The proprietor says a helmet like the one Jake borrowed, covered in black felt and shaped like a bowl, offers more protection than the aerodynamic plastic helmets which, to me, look more manly. I associate bowl helmets with effete riders jumping over hedges after foxes. But when we bump back down the steps, we've got an effete helmet in a box, and he's wearing stylish, black riding boots that zip tight and snug. I've got his orthotics and clunky shoes in a bag.

The neon Budweiser sign lures me toward the restaurant. I bump him up more steps to an outdoor table where we can look over pickup trucks, horse trailers, dust, and an amazing variety of haunches. I hold a straw to Jake's lips as he sips Guava Berry Vita Boost from his lunch pack. With the other hand I tilt a long-necked bottle of Bud to my own parched lips.

"Well, Jake, that trotting is something, isn't it?"

It's okay.

"Blue's a nice horse … pony, eh?"

You ought to be up there on that saddle.

"You did good, kid."

Out in the arena, I see a familiar figure riding a horse that seems huge, perhaps because she is small. It's the instructor's disabled daughter. She has a riding crop and is whacking the animal for some disobedience invisible to my eye. On horseback, there's no way to tell she has such trouble walking. She's in complete control, fearless, erect, urging the horse forward at what I now recognize as a trot, and her bowed-in knees seem an advantage clasping the horse's neck. She's a perfect example of a predator controlling prey.

A pickup pulls up to the restaurant—a clattering diesel Ram—and a man in broken-down boots, wearing jeans, a work shirt and a cowboy hat gets out. He strides up onto the deck checking out Jake in his riding boots and wheelchair. Then he looks at me in sandals and shit brown socks.

"Howdy," he says,

"Howdy."

The disabled girl continues circling the arena on a huge horse that seems quite obedient. My own predator-in-training is tired and ready for home.

"Well, Jake, same time next week?

He opens his mouth wide: *Sure, Dad, you bet.*

I drain my beer, pack his juice, and we bump back down the steps.

Simulacrum

IT'S ONE OF THOSE MOMENTS that you can watch developing, like a Polaroid. On the kitchen table is Jake's wooden farm puzzle: barn, goat, lamb, pig, tractor, dog, goose, hen, and pony with two bareback riders. It's a classic child's puzzle from that faraway time of mythic virtues before corporate farming. Whatever these plywood cutouts represent to Jake is anyone's guess, but it's been his favorite for a long time, like comfort food, and every so often he asks for it again by looking yearningly at the shelf beside the table.

A wooden peg on each piece of the farm allowed it to be pulled from the board and, more important, put back in place. In Jake's case the pegs let his clumsy fingers drag a piece from board, and since he lacked the coordination and hand control to put it back, to do the next best thing, whip it onto the floor so that whoever was present would have to pick it up and put it back in place.

He never tired of the game, but pretty soon I began malingering, waiting for all nine pieces to fall before restoring the family farm, and being sure to groan as I picked up each piece. He thought it was part of the game. He liked it even better if I hid in the next room and then called for a particular puzzle piece. Feigning excitement, I'd rush back, and he'd be all scrunched up laughing at a pig on the floor. I'd massage his tight shoulders to make him laugh even harder.

This day I'm herding dirty dishes from one counter to another, mopping whatever portion of revealed counter seems most nauseating, and heating spaghetti water while moving Delta talker and keyboard off the table, backpack to a chair. I kick a pile of clothes off the bedroom floor, put the towel that Jake lies on after his morning bath over the shower rod alongside the towel he gets dried with, alongside my own towel. How many days towels can be reused is a question that has never yet been satisfactorily answered.

Back chopping garlic, onions and tomatoes I realize that nine puzzle pieces have taken a very long time to hit the floor today. Perhaps he's daydreaming about the young Basque woman who put him in a stander (to provide weight bearing and proper hip development) while playing with this very puzzle on a tray attached to the stander. I've thought about her often, and now, whenever there is another explosion or arrest in Spain, I wonder if she is all right.

Fingers reeking of onions and garlic, I look over Jake's shoulder. The pig, lamb, dog, goat, tractor, and hen lie scattered on the floor. Jake looks up, wanting my attention. I assume he wants another sip of Guava Berry Vita Boost and hold the straw to his lips. He sips, pulls up the barn, and I'm pleased that he can drink through a straw and pluck at the same time. He's getting coordinated after a fashion.

But something's up. He keeps looking from the puzzle to me and back. Still I don't get it. Only the goose and pony remain. Then I get it—a pale *yellow* pony!

"It's Blue!" I exclaim.

A dazzling full-wattage smile tells me I'm on the track.

"And that's you on Blue."

His face scrunches with delight, just as it did under his effete helmet on the real pale pony. But he's not done. He pulls out the pony and pushes it to the side of the table, the usual launching point for the floor. He glances at me with an odd quizzical expression and then, instead of pushing the pony off the edge, he moves it to safer ground. The gesture is absolutely clear.

He cares about this pony. This boy who has never cared for stuffed animals, not even the zebra watching over his eighteen days in the NICU as death became rebirth. I loved that zebra. But Jake, whether they are in his crib, on his bed, on shelves or tables, cares little for stuffed animals. Now he's so desperate to communicate about a plywood horse that he succeeds.

Yesterday, we'd taken carrots to Blue, and I'd held his fingers around a carrot as we stood in front of an amiable animal who, suddenly, pulled back her lips and lunged with huge yellow teeth, frightening us both.

"She's hungry," the instructor said. " It's time for her dinner."

Jake was on the verge of crying.

"Blue is hungry, that's all," I said. "Nothing to be afraid of." Although those yellow teeth at the end of a long jaw had looked huge compared to a small hand.

The instructor demonstrated a better way to hold a carrot, flat on her palm. Sure enough, Blue's big rubbery lips whisked it away into crunching sounds. Since it's difficult for Jake to extend a flat palm, I try it myself, and the lips feel good as the carrot vanishes.

That was yesterday. Now, staring at the wooden horse and riders, I translate his expression: *I know what it means to ride like these kids painted on a piece of wood, which is only a simulacrum for the real thing.*

To emphasize his point, Jake plucks the goose, the last farm animal left, and whips it off the table onto the floor, leaving the plywood horse safely to the side. He looks up mischievously.

Got it, Dad? He grins.

Got it, son. I grin at his grin, while tearing up. Discreet tears, of course, in order not to alarm him.

The farm is scattered on the floor, except for the horse and two children riding bareback. That piece sits beside nine empty holes of the puzzle board. It's humid inside the kitchen from boiling water. The smell of simmering garlic and marinara and onions and ground beef reaches into my stomach the way seeing a carrot must have reached into Blue's stomach. Instead of lunging, however, I get up in a dignified manner, drop some pasta into boiling water, and wipe my eyes. While far away over the mountains, in her evening stall, Blue breathes through her big soft nostrils.

Which she won't be doing much longer because an incurable disease will cause her to be euthanized. But for us she lives. In this very puzzle. In orthotic boots from Poland inspired by his riding boots, and in this chair where he's sitting. After seeing him on Blue's saddle, I recognized the perfect chair at an office supply—a saddle chair. It stretches hamstrings, transfers weight to his feet, arches his back, keep his hips from further surgery, and keeps him out of a wheelchair. Also it looks cool. So Blue lives on as Jake rides through his days.

Power to the People

WE'RE HEADING FOR a power wheelchair trial at California Children's Services—Jake and Mom in the new van, me running late in the Honda that we bought before Jake was born, back when I was still righteous about simplicity. Power-assisted windows, seats, locks, mirrors? No way. Power makes you lazy. Power saps strength, leads to decadence and loss of authenticity. Soon you can do nothing for yourself. And then, when the power fails, you are helpless. Besides, manual was cheaper. Five years later the van has power everything, and I've succumbed to TV, dishwasher, cell phone, all the while knowing they are like foxtails in a dog's paw. They'll work through a man and emerge in pus at the far side.

It's obvious that power is Jake's future. Look at his communication device and computer. A power chair will enhance his *proprioception*, a new word for me. It's what the highway patrol tests by having you close your eyes and touch your nose. It's the awareness of your body in space, that we can only learn by moving our bodies through space. The power chair is supposed to do that for Jake. Also it will give him independence, what toddlers learn by running into the street.

This is our fourth attempt. The first trial was a flop. We were supposed to wait in a room full of fun stuff—paints, balloons, bubbles—none of which Jake could do or wanted to do. Communal activities distress him as much as they do me. At his age I'd do anything to avoid pinning the tail on the donkey. His only recourse was crying, which he did with such gusto that I took him outside while Mom chatted with his new therapist, a young woman who had replaced the man from Reno.

When it was our turn, the purveyor of the power chair, a dominatrix, commanded Jake to use the joystick in ways that were impossible given his lack of coordination. He has only two responses to bullying: to scream or slump. He slumped, and I did the screaming.

"This isn't working," I told her. "He needs a quiet place to play by himself." After all, play led to walking and biking. "Let's try it outside."

"I can't let you go alone," she said. "I need to be there."

"Well, this won't work."

I didn't like her, she didn't like me, and the new therapist didn't know either of us well enough to intervene. "Okay," the wheelchair woman said finally, "but only in the play yard, with you and no one else."

Using the joystick, I drove Jake to the play yard where disabled kids were having a fine noisy time in plastic houses and on slides. He slumped until they went back to class. Only then, when we were alone, did he try the joystick with splayed fingers or the back of his hand. He spun circles on the Astroturf with something like intent, jerked forward and backward. The joystick seemed possible until the dominatrix summoned the chair for another child.

Our next trial had a different wheelchair rep, the good one we were assured. This time Jake's teachers from the Bridge School came to watch. They were excited by the prospect of his mobility, and at their suggestion, three switches had been attached to a plastic tray affixed to the chair. The switches, familiar from school, were easy to press with a clumsy hand, yellow forward, blue right, green left. It was an ingenious and promising arrangement I thought, but with parents, therapist, teachers waiting for him to perform, he began to scream. I took him to the car. When we came back, decisions had been made. He would operate a power chair by tapping switches. But not those on a tray. He'd use his head to tap switches embedded in his headrest. His teachers, Mom, the new therapist and the good wheelchair woman had made an executive decision. Jake had good head control at school.

"If you'd give him a decent chance with his hands," I pleaded, "you might be surprised."

But no, the boy who bestrode the therapy center on Mondays and Wednesdays, bashing bolsters and leading his therapist on a wheeled stool, the boy who rode a low-rider bicycle around town, would now be strapped into a power chair, a head on wheels, hands helpless appendages. I felt the way he must when decisions were made for him—helpless. Impotent. And angry. If the therapist from Reno hadn't quit to write the novel I had encouraged, Kung Fu would have slain these demons.

Next visit, sure enough, Jake was strapped into a support vest, knees bound with a winding of straps, feet strapped in, looking like a mummy. But, banging his head, he was causing the chair to turn left or right, or go straight ahead. This was deemed good progress. For me, watching a boy so physically and spiritually alive, banging his head at a machine that engulfed him made me blind with despair.

"He's really taking to it," his new therapist said. "Amazing."

I loved the adjective, but what I saw was more akin to the electric chair—Jake bound in place and waiting for the power. I knew my resistance to power was stupid and that I was being truculent. But knowing only made me more so. How could a man dumbly flipping TV stations oppose head switches serving a far better end? Hypocrisy did not improve my mood.

So today, driving toward yet another power chair trial, I'm working on my attitude: Power is inevitable and irresistible. You think those twisted-up kids in India wouldn't love power? Foxtails for you, maybe, but wings for Jake.

I arrive to find him strapped into the power chair. He smiles gamely at me, bangs his head, the chair turns. He bangs again, and the chair goes ahead. He's getting the idea, doing what's asked, but without the excitement of bashing bolsters or speeding down hills. His mom is looking pleased. Her ex, who dislikes himself for driving when he could walk, for watching *NYPD Blue* when he could read, for letting software correct his spelling, and for talking on a cell phone while traveling at high speed, looks on glumly.

Power is neutral, I remind myself. Use is the issue. Sure the country is drunk on power. But those poor Iraqis on the Highway of Death underestimated the power of technology and were fried to a crisp. Technology reigns. Power liberates. Power is good. Think wings not foxtails.

When Jake and his mom leave in the power-everything van, I unlock the Honda with an actual key. The Honda does have after-market air conditioning because it was soon obvious that the car's design, dramatically-angled front and rear windows, made it intolerable on just a warm day. About the time Iraqis were being burned alive in desert heat, I succumbed to air conditioning … for Jake's sake of course. Because an infant would roast in that car.

Now, having capitulated to power, I'm dealing with my Phantom Geezer, who is unconvinced: *You know the hard way is the good way. Forget Iraqis. When the power fails, who will remember celestial navigation? The garage door won't open, brakes won't work, you're trapped in the elevator. And when you drive into the lake, car windows won't open. You're helpless.*

I slam the steering wheel (no power assist). *Fuck you, Geezer! You want to beat your clothes on the rocks? Go ahead! You're talking to the wrong man about decadence and the devil's work. I love my power screwdriver. And I'm not ashamed to admit it. Power is good. Power liberates. Even the fucking cell phone. I love it.*

Hot air whips through the driver-side window. It's getting so hard to roll up or down that I often don't. *Try opening **that** underwater*, I say. I turn on the air-con to spite him.

See, the Geezer says, *this is what happens.*

Just shut up!

He does. In silence, we continue down the freeway at our customary speed, seventy miles per hour, scooping up warm air, mixing it with cool, and sending it back out the open window.

The North Face of Safeway

FOR YEARS I RESISTED handicapped parking, who needs the stigma, we'd do it on our own, but these days the blue handicapped sign with the wheelchair icon glows like a martini at the end of the day. I pull up in front of Safeway, kill the engine and slump awhile. I dread getting him into his collapsible wheelchair that looks like an infant stroller. Around the house I assist his walking, around town he rides his bike, but now he will become an infant. That may explain what happens next. Either that or Mallory's reason for climbing Everest: *Because it's there*.

I unslump and turn to the backseat. "Want to try walking in today?"

Our walking involves me standing behind him, torquing his shoulders so his legs won't cross, while at the same time helping shift his weight forward. After long practice, I'm the only person who can do it.

His open-mouthed *yes* is so vigorous that he grunts for emphasis. He doesn't need speech to register enthusiasm. I open the rear sliding door, swing his legs out of the van, get him on his feet without fully considering what's involved. It's the way we begin many of our adventures: just get started and then deal with whatever happens. In his black riding boots and red bandana he cuts quite a dashing figure. Evidently he thinks so, too, because he sets off by himself on scissoring legs, and I have to lunge to prevent a fall.

Once positioned behind him with both hands on his shoulders, we begin our dance (as his new physical therapist calls it). We head for the pressure mat that opens the entrance door to Safeway, a door we've been through many times in the wheelchair, but this time, on foot, he freezes when the door wheezes open, body rigid, head turned toward the door, opposing arm flung the other way. It's called *fixing* in therapy speak. A Feldenkrais practitioner thought it resulted from being strangled in utero. But we've dropped Feldenkrais, conductive education, acupressure, homeopathy, osteopathy, and now it's just a kid in a red bandana striking something like a modern dance pose on the pressure mat of Safeway and causing me to stumble, and the woman behind us to stop.

"Don't do that, Jake," I admonish, "or we'll both do a face plant."

Admonishing is my thing, and he laughs. No doubt he finds the phrase "face plant" funny, although I've told him what a fall would mean, how instead of reaching out to break his fall, his hands would pull back reflexively, and he'd hit the floor face first with his 215-pound father on top of him. But our close calls make no impression. He's quite certain I'll never let him fall.

Annoyed by his laughter, I hoist him bodily into the store (so much for walking) and let the woman pass. She does with a sympathetic smile … also with a grocery cart. Big oversight! How do I keep two hands on Jake and carry groceries? And just that fast we're in triage mode. Diapers. The only essential item is diapers. I should be able to tuck them under one arm … unless … the thought is too humiliating … unless I ask for help. But that's a slippery slope best avoided. Once you start, where do you stop? Help is out of the question.

As we find our walking rhythm, I chart the most direct course to diapers, but he stops, body rigid, head craned to the left. It's the ice cream aisle. As motivation for walking, he gets to stop where he wants, so admonishment is out of the question. But my armpits are prickly, a full sweat not far off, and it's hard to tell which of us is more tense.

"I can't carry any ice cream today," I say.

A reason, even a good one, means nothing. He continues to twist toward ice cream while I torque him toward diapers. I can feel his reproach, *So much for going where I want to go.* But I'm stronger (at least for the next few years) and I'm thinking of just one thing: getting out of Safeway alive. I nudge him down the aisle toward diapers where, it's immediately evident, economy-size is way too bulky to tuck under my arm. Pausing for deliberation does not please him. He registers that fact with a grunting sound, and when I tuck the smallest diaper pack under my arm and turn toward checkout, he cranes toward deli. If he can't do the freezer aisle, then by god he wants deli.

"Jake, next time we'll just walk around the store for fun. Okay?"

We both know it's an unlikely promise, and his physical annoyance now becomes a rumbling sound, not unlike a dog's warning. Translation: *I don't want checkout.* This is not a good moment because a battle of wills brings out the worst in both of us. I'm actually sweating now, and with diapers under my arm, walking is even more difficult, an excellent excuse for quick departure.

"It's a long way back to the car, Jake, we need to leave."

Like a cop with a prisoner, I frog-march him to the end of the line. The kid ahead of us is wearing tattoos and baggy pants, some kind of huge shoes, a muscle shirt, a reversed ball cap. He's a stringy-muscled punk in the new ugly mode who glances back at us with an expression I recognize: *Hey, that kid is crippled.*

That kid is also rumbling toward shriek, my great fear in public places. Shirley the check-out woman is dutifully running items over the scanner for a lady intending to pay by check. The woman writes slowly, admiring her handiwork as if balancing her checkbook, and Shirley looks grim.

Jake screeches. It's a sound perfected over eight years that cuts through Muzak and eardrums. People at every check-stand turn in alarm. Even punk is startled out of his persona and turns in surprise. Shirley stops scanning and looks up. This screech would cause his mother to take him home for a *time out*, a term that annoys me. I prefer: *Goddamn it, Jake, do that one more time and we're going home.* But we're trapped on foot with no easy way out, and Jake knows it. I can read his thoughts like Braille. *You want to shove me around, let's see how you like the screech.*

And he's got the upper hand. My only recourse is parental sternness which, as he well knows, is aimed as much at audience as him. "That's enough, Jake."

I can feel him processing possibilities: *Dad is definitely more irascible and punitive than Mom, and he did walk me in here. So, okay, I'll let it go at one screech. This time.*

He relaxes.

I soften my grip.

Shirley goes back to scanning.

Punk goes back to surly.

And check-writing-lady actually smiles at us: *Imagine that! One word from his father and the boy shuts up, unlike these women who bribe kids with candy. Too bad the boy's crippled.*

I'm actually pretty impressed myself.

When our diapers finally reach her end of the conveyor belt, Shirley's mood has not changed. She shoves the package across the scanner, drops it into a plastic bag, and says, "Do you want help out?" It's such an obvious solution to my dilemma that I can't accept.

"We're fine," I say.

So we set off with bagged diapers hanging from my arm and banging Jake's shoulder. When he doesn't stop on the pressure mat, I'm thinking we've done it! We walked Safeway! But then he does stop outside, and it takes a moment to see the reason. Parked beside our handicapped space is the yellow Hummer I've spent the past year loathing as *a piece of shit, a goddamn gas hog desecrating its*

American flag decal. But Jake loves big vehicles—and yellow! He couldn't be happier in his dance pose, twisting toward the shiny yellow wall.

Since he won't move, I have to drag him to the van, taking care to register my annoyance with extra brusque handling. I hoist him into the car seat, and only when we're on the road, windows down, sweat drying, do I manage to ask his opinion of our expedition.

"Well," I say, "that was quite an adventure, wasn't it?"

His open-mouthed *yes* is so hugely enthusiastic that I translate: *It sure was, Pop. Let's do it again soon.*

"We'll do it again … sometime soon."

We both know what that pause means. I'm equivocating. But the farther from Safeway, the better the adventure looks, and pretty soon I'm considering our next expedition with a backpack.

"You did great, kid. I think that's our longest walk … ever."

His expressive face replies: *Piece of cake, Dad. Only next time, how about a little less admonishment?*

Maniacs

SOMETIMES IT'S HARD TO TELL when a turning point occurs. After the farm puzzle came the alphabet board, also suitable for toddlers. The letters of the alphabet had slightly raised edges to pull them out, and that, as his therapist would say, required fine motor control. He was sitting in one of my contraptions of the moment (before Blue's chair), wavering like a tree in a windstorm. Still, he managed to drag his fingers over the puzzle surface until they caught a letter, a little like raking leaves. Then he'd sweep that letter, or several if he was lucky, onto the floor with a vigorous backhanded swipe. Twenty-six small letters whipped into a room at high velocity can be difficult to find. Which was fine with him.

He was becoming deliberate about which letter he chose, and to test that theory I went into farm-puzzle mode, hiding in the next room and calling, this time, for a *B* rather than a *barn*. A piece hit the floor. I rushed in prepared to praise whatever letter he'd pulled up.

He was sitting, arms cocked like a typist or pianist (if you didn't know that a non-progressive lesion of the brain was causing over-tight muscles to cock his arms that way), and looking down at the floor.

At the letter *B*.

"Amazing," I said.

The ensuing praise, extravagant even by my standards, worked us both into a frenzy of excitement. For many days we played alphabet before I tried another toddler's game, flip-up keys where you pressed a key and a flap would open revealing a picture. *P* gave you *pig*, *Y* gave you *yo-yo*. The keys were small like the alphabet board, but he was determined, and before long he was popping up pigs and yo-yos with a clicking sound reminiscent of an actual keyboard.

"Tell you what, Jake, I've got an idea."

He gave me a wary look, since my notion of good ideas did not always mesh with his.

"How about a different game?"

He delivered *the look*. Translation: *I don't like different. What's wrong with this game?*

Despite his resistance, I sat him in front of the little-used computer in his bedroom, and his body tightened with a warning whine. He knew I was up to no good. What I had in mind was using the keyboard the Bridge School had abandoned in favor of a head-mounted laser pointer. The keyboard had a Plexiglas cover with a hole over each letter, making it easier for spastic fingers to isolate a single key. We'd sent it to the shelf of abandoned technology, and he was not happy at its reappearance.

The letters are larger than what he's been doing and, to my eye, much easier to manipulate, but it's a delicate moment, a tipping point, because a full-blown tantrum will end this project. I wait in silence while he considers his degree of outrage. Finally, almost accidentally, he sticks a finger through a hole in the Plexiglas. A letter appears on screen. The computer speaks the letter. He listens. He presses another key. Soon there's a string of letters on the screen, and he's listening to his keystrokes like a pianist noodling.

"If you hit *enter*," I say, "it'll say all the letters."

He knows what the *enter* key will do from school and now one of his fingers finds the *enter* hole. Out spills a cacophony of sounds—his keyboard composition—and he laughs with surprise and delight as I rub his tight shoulders and plot my next move.

"Want me to hide and call you a letter?"

He gives me a huge, open-mouthed *yes*, which means that we've successfully segued from farm puzzle to alphabet puzzle to pop-up game to high-tech keyboard. I hide in the kitchen.

"How about an *X*?" I call out. It's an easy letter for him to reach.

Silence. A long silence. Then a computer voice says "*X*," and I rush in for a back-rub and laugh. We play at single letters. Then two letters. No problem. Then three letters. We're both laughing hysterically, but for different reasons. He's happy in the moment, I'm looking ahead.

"Shall we tell them at school you're using the keyboard? We can put it on your recorder for class tomorrow."

His body language couldn't be clearer: *No, no, please not.*

I well understand fear of failure. *If you tell, they'll expect me to do it, and then I could fail.*

"Okay," I say, "we'll wait till you say it's okay."

Of course that's what I said about trike-riding but blabbed to his teacher (the same teacher who gave us *sad* and woke to a night of terror). "We're working on a secret," I told her, hoping my vagueness would conceal betrayal.

"Oh," she replied, "we already know the secret. Mom told us about the trike."

So, despite living in separate houses with scant communication, Mom and Dad had become Little League parents advertising their son's success against his wishes.

There's worse to come. I figure if he's doing three letters, spelling his name would be fun (and educational to boot). Pretending they are random, I call out the letters, *J-A-K-E*, but when the computer speaks his name and I rush in, he's frozen in shock, almost as if struck. Then he starts to cry.

And it's quite clear: I have become a Little League Monster. Of course, hearing a computer say your name might give anyone the *fantods*, as Huck would say. Poor Huck. Poor us. In which case, that makes it the computer's fault, not mine. Chastened, I renounce deception while he noodles himself back to good cheer.

From here on, I think, everything will be on the up and up. Next day, I say: "Want to try some vowels, Jake?" Vowels have been drummed into him at school on picture boards and with his head pointer and at one time on this keyboard, and his whine of protest couldn't be clearer. *This is a game, not school. No. Absolutely not. N. O.*

A Little League father, even one in recovery, can't capitulate so easily. What I'll do, I decide, is revise my ethical guidelines. If vowels are good for you, like fiber in your diet, they'll still be good for you if you don't call them vowels. A letter is just a letter. My conscience is clear.

Back in hiding, I call for an *E.*

When the computer says "*E,*" I pounce with an enthusiastic back rub, producing screams of delight.

Then I call for an *I.*

"*I*" says the computer, followed by hysterical laughter and back rub.

"Give me an *O.*"

"Give me a *U.*"

Finally, I call out "*A.*"

"*A*" the computer echoes.

If I'd begun with *A* he might have smelled a rat but, given *EIOUA*, he doesn't smell a rat, thereby completing his vowels and providing me a triumph akin to watching your kid strike out a dangerous batter or hit a home run. My kid. Me. My son, hitting five out of five vowels without a miss, a feat that would have seemed impossible a few days ago, is batting 1000.

A new nickname springs to my lips, nonsense nicknames being our specialty. "You're just a keyboard maniac."

He smiles because my tone suggests other superlatives— *amazing, fabulous, outstanding, excellent*—which, though well worn, are still welcome. Where *maniac* comes from in the current context, god knows. His current nickname, *Punk,* derived from *Punkin,* which came from *Dunkin Punkin,* which came from *Mr.*

Pumpkin, which may have had something to do with Halloween. Or perhaps not. They come and go, the nicknames.

Now the *maniac* puts his head down, stabbing keys faster than I thought possible. *BZKLLQQDTTXXX*.

He looks up with a grin, presses *enter*. The entire collection of letters clatters from the computer in a way that makes us both laugh. He gives me his significant look, an intense expression meaning that something of particular import is up. But what? I look at him. He looks at the screen. I look at the screen. He hits *enter*. Out come the letters. All consonants.

And then I get it. He isn't noodling, he's performing a premeditated attack on vowels.

"Jake," I say, laughing. "You *are* a maniac!"

Confident that he's got me where he wants me, he adds a few more consonants, not a vowel in sight, and hits *enter* (which, until a few days ago, was a remarkable feat in itself).

Then again.

And again.

It's his own Little League game—for fathers.

And we're both laughing like maniacs.

Let this be the turning point.

If

JAKE'S IN HIS BEDROOM having a tantrum that would drive me into punishment mode. That's why I'm not in the bedroom. The Tibetan woman is. She won't capitulate, or get pissed off, and it's taken Jake awhile to realize that. Other caregivers—Russian, Costa Rican, Brazilian, Hungarian, Slovak, Mexican, Basque, Burmese, Indian—have been more malleable.

Not the Tibetan. She speaks four languages: Hindi, Tibetan, Japanese, English, helped found a school for disabled Tibetan children in India, is active in the Free Tibet movement. And may be thirty. In exchange for twelve hours work with Jake each week, she moved into our guest room and became my ally in liberating Jake's hands.

Whether my stubborn resistance to the school's advice is smart or stupid I no longer know, but instinctive resistance is my mode. His mom, on the other hand, believes that if the best school of its kind in the country decides to use a head pointer with icons on a talker, why waste time practicing keyboard skills? Why *not* use a wheelchair? Why insist on toileting? Face reality. Your son is severely disabled.

I do wonder about my motives: Am I pushing Jake because I want him to be as much like other kids as possible? Is that why I resist ugly wheelchairs and orthotics? Why I push walking and sitting at tables, riding a bike, using the toilet? Is that why I resist a head pointer, flip charts and icons recommended by the best school of its kind? Because a keyboard is more *normal*? Because, at his age, all I wanted was *normal* (or as we say these days, *typical*), because I myself felt completely abnormal. Is that why I want a tutor like the Tibetan woman that you might hire for a *typical* nine-year-old? Which, of course, he is not. Nor, at his age, was I.

I make a video of them working together. She reads sentences aloud and he types them, slowly, with difficulty, but he can use the keyboard and also loves spelling the words she reads to him.

When his Bridge teacher sees the video, she agrees. "You win," she says returning the keyboard to school routine.

However, our victory further divides Jake's two homes, and his mom, disinclined to hook keyboard to computer, sticks with the head pointer. But our acrimony is obliterated by catastrophe.

In March 2001 his teachers arrange a meeting to discuss transition. We've always known that someday Jake would leave the Bridge School, his shelter and ours from the world. Someday. But not yet. Not now. Tactfully, his teachers suggest that he may be ready for transition in the fall.

"But," we say, "he has no preferred communication mode, no dependable toileting mode. When he sits in classes at the neighboring elementary school, he becomes disruptive. No way is he ready!"

Well, they say, *if* he were to transition, what grade would be appropriate?

Well, *if* he were to transition, he's old enough for third grade. On the other hand, he's young, small for his age, as I was. My mother held me back. So perhaps second grade might be best.

And *if* he transitioned, to what school would that be?

Well, since you've heard (endlessly) about his father's old elementary school, and what a great school it was, and about his bike rides there, and since Dad's house is in the district, how about there?

Well, *if* so, and *if* you want full inclusion, it would be necessary to contact them.

Now Jake who, depending on whom you ask, cannot walk or sit; who may, depending, be continent, or not; who may use a computer in a somewhat normal, that is to say typical mode, or not; who can, no question about it, eject himself screaming from any classroom … that boy will now go to public school, not just any school, but his father's beloved elementary school, Las Lomas.

Which, if that is possible, is less prepared for his arrival than we are for departure from the Bridge School. Las Lomas has no experience with a kid in a wheelchair, much less one who cannot speak. The principal is sufficiently unpleasant that even Jake's mom, more generous in her assessment of people than I am, dislikes this man. Truculently (he has no legal choice) he calls an official Individualized Education Program meeting, where Jake's educational plan for the coming year will be determined.

His assigned teacher is not present when the IEP meeting begins. County support staff for the disabled are there, as are three current teachers from the Bridge School intending to explain Jake's communication methods, motivational difficulties, and various devices. Several school staff are present, exhausted toward the end of a school year, and not much interested in this additional burden. No one has heard of a Vanguard talker activated by laser, had experience with an adapted keyboard that will attach to a computer, if one were available, understands why it might be difficult to sit at a table in a wheelchair, or, recommended by Dad, without one. None of these people has the faintest idea how a speechless kid will participate in class. Neither do his parents. But we have hope.

When his assigned teacher finally arrives, visibly unhappy at not being consulted about this meeting, there is no room for her to sit. She was assigned this kid because no other teacher would accept him, and her principal has done nothing to prepare her. A chair is found and hostilities break out between her and the outsiders. She is told that an adaptive PE teacher, present in the room, will be invading her class during PE, and so will a speech language specialist from the county.

Even worse are strangers from the Bridge School talking about appropriate seating in *her* classroom. They talk about communication devices and a full inclusion aide (who doesn't exist) in her classroom. His father and mother talk as if, like any other student, their son belongs in her class. The father even thinks his own attendance at this school fifty years ago is relevant and, oh, by the way, his mother also taught here.

He seems to think his son, whom she has never laid eyes on, will sit in an adapted chair at a table with other students. (She doesn't have tables.) He talks about his son using a special keyboard connected to a computer. (What computer?) There's even talk about diaper changes. And, oh, yes, as if all these devices, pointers, charts, aides and diapers weren't enough, the boy can be disruptive in class. (In her second grade class there are *no* disruptions.) And despite all this, they are talking about how smart he is.

"I may sound negative," she says, "but *positive negativism* is my way of heading off problems." Which she sees nothing but. Clearly, this boy has no place at an elite elementary school serving some of the wealthiest families in the country. Aren't there county programs to keep kids like this out of sight?

But his parents have visited such programs, as required by law, and found them unsuitable. *Unsuitable* is a euphemism. We found county programs so demoralizing that, for the first time in the two years since she left the house, his mother and I were in complete agreement. No way would Jake sit in a room of disabled kids waiting to be old enough to be excluded, legally, from public education. Our unanimous choice was full inclusion in public school. However, inclusion in *this* school was my choice, and the atmosphere in this room is beyond hostile.

After the meeting, we sit with the Bridge School teachers at a nearby café where Jake and I stop on bike rides. We have come to know and trust these teachers over the past three years, and we are anxious to hear their opinion of what just happened, hoping for reassurance of the sort they've so generously provided.

They do try. Transitions, they say, are always difficult, but finally, pressed by our desperation, they admit that it was the worst transition meeting they have ever experienced.

For the first time, I understand what Jake faces in the real world. I look at his mom. She seems dazed.

I look at teachers who love him and are unable to smile. My progressive school filled with freewheeling individualists—teachers and students alike—where my mother would have welcomed Jake into her chaotic classroom, has vanished.

Sitting in glum silence, I watch traffic pass on the street where I rode my bike to school. I try to imagine Jake on this street, leaning back, legs stretched out like Peter Fonda on his chopper. But that film was 1969. Jake will ride into September, 2001.

Stricken, not knowing what to say, his parents and current teachers can barely meet one another's eyes. His teachers stand. They will go back to the classroom where Jake is working wit h aides and his talker. I'll pick him up after school for a bike ride. But we won't be visiting this café on the Alameda de las Pulgas.

Not today.

The Turd's Tale

SOONER OR LATER it is necessary to talk about shit. Not poop or doo doo or BMs or number 2, but shit. And that time has come. The Twin Towers are down. There is shit everywhere in the country, and Jake is in second grade at the school I came to from Reno and Stockton as one of those kids who, when you make a sociogram, no arrows run from him to anyone else, and no arrows run from anyone else to him, a kid who shuffled around playgrounds avoiding groups. Now he recited *The Cremation of Sam Magee* to the combined 7th–8th grade, got his hand up at mental math before anyone else, wrote stories about subs and jungle warfare in the recent war, and swarmed out of the old Victorian onto a grassy field for disorganized play.

I even had a friend. Then two. And when I graduated, I was confident enough to disdain high school—clubs, sports, hot rods, rock and roll—the works. If smoking was popular, I didn't smoke. Likewise (despite my bloodline) I abstained from booze. Better to reject than be rejected. There was a direct line between Las Lomas and Reed College where, in the crew-cut fifties, it was possible to reject the entire decade. Rejection is in my blood.

Jake's bike ride to school is along a road familiar from fifty years ago, but far more dangerous. Cars as big as those of the fifties, but far uglier, pass like military vehicles in a convoy, but a convoy lacking military discipline. Since there are still no sidewalks, we go against traffic. I steer from his right side, where I can glare at oncoming drivers. The Alameda de las Pulgas is a dangerous place.

Twice each day we pass the vanished house of my best friend (dead at twenty-two) whose parents served as my surrogate family. We pass what was once the Economy Market, now a Starbucks. We pass the last recognizable relic of memory, a funky grocery where, I tell Jake, my mother shopped on her way home from teaching third grade at Las Lomas. I don't mention the sherry she bought or her death certificate that, three years before Jake's birth, listed cirrhosis as the cause of her death.

She wouldn't have recognized a school no longer the Summerhill of California, free-wheeling and innovative. Now parents expect education as rigorous as that dispensed by nuns, English headmasters, or a military academy. There is no place for a disruptive kid in a wheelchair who arrives on a weird low-rider bike steered by a father who, rumor has it, is angry at the school.

Truculence reigns. When his aide calls for me to pick up Jake, again, after being ejected from class, I get angry at the school that had taught me not to conform. Worse, I get mad at him for not conforming. His aide, a tall Russian woman who will soon return to Russia, is also angry at Jake's treatment, but complaining to me is her only recourse. That and not coming to school at all. On this November day, 2001, she is absent.

Law requires a substitute aide, but there is none, so I will be spending the day in class. We are met by his teacher who does not greet me, nor do I greet her. Instead, she leans over Jake, still strapped into his low-rider bike with a helmet on his head, and hisses: "You *will* behave in my class."

According to his aide this teacher is wound so tight she's near breakdown, and I can believe it now, her face twisted with anger in the presence of a man who, she may or may not know, has requested a different teacher. The principal refused. She turns away. I'm so stunned, I say nothing. Does this happen every morning?

So our day begins. Transferring him into his wheelchair, I feel Jake wind up like a steel spring, and I'm just as tight because of my own culpability in this ugly situation. From the aide, I know he is required to sit behind other students near the door, ready for ejection. He may participate with his Vanguard talker, using his fingers rather than head pointer, but he's slow and will rarely perform on command. More likely he types a word (I'm still amazed that he can do it) that the machine says aloud, often at an inappropriate time. Which is all day. Some days he manages to sit passively; other days he's wheeled as far from class as possible, behind the backboards near the vanished creek, and I'm called to pick him up.

We sit behind students at individual desks. A student goes to the board for an arithmetic lesson; other students make hand signals to agree or disagree with the results. Speech is not tolerated. At a school once noisy with students working together, absolute silence and absolute attention to the teacher are now required. The school ranks among the best in the state. The first week, she warned her second grade students about year-end tests. "Don't worry," she told them, "I will prepare you."

As a result, terror rules. From the principal down. If corporal punishment were permissible, this school would be the place for it, and I'm back in my second grade classroom beside the Truckee River in Reno, too shy to make friends or respond in class, feeling isolated, shunned. I *felt* shunned and cowed. But Jake, sitting beside me slumped over his speaking device in his wheelchair, really *is* shunned. However, he won't be cowed. When his compromised nervous system can't abide this penal colony any longer, he demands release.

I can hear it coming and look at the teacher conducting her lesson. She's avoiding looking at Jake or me. So I lean toward him, trying to prevent a breakdown, and whisper the first thing that comes to mind: "Two plus two equals what?"

She hears my whisper. Jake groans. I stand up. She stares over the heads of students who, risking penalty for disobedience, turn their heads. What they see is a sixty-six-year-old man butting the classroom door open and pulling his son's wheelchair backwards from the room.

"Do not leave this room," she says sharply, her face a rictus. Like my own, I expect.

Jake looks up at me, silent, surprised, not knowing what to expect. That makes two of us. I exchange wheelchair for bike and I walk beside him the mile home. In the past, I might have banished him to bed, but on this day we lie together. What does he think about what just happened? What is he thinking about the past three months of rejection and anger? Whatever, he's happy now. It's his father, lying beside him, who's being punished by his own dark thoughts.

Since we now have an entire school day still ahead, I suggest an afternoon swim at Bill's house. Retired from teaching fiction writing at the university where I was his student, he keeps his outdoor pool warm at this time of year, and we often swim there, nude, Jake happy to be released from a diaper into warm water.

The possibility of swimming causes Jake to wriggle with excitement and shriek, but I'm so depressed that by the time we get to the pool, I can barely get Jake undressed and into his life vest and swim fins. Happy to be floating on his back in a warm pool on a chill November day, he kicks to the other end of the pool and into *the jungle*. That is to say, overhanging philodendron and loquat branches that conceal leopards, monkeys, anacondas and hippos. He bumps to a stop beneath the canopy.

For three months I've allowed school complaints and humiliations to fester, the better to maintain my own rage and denial. Bill has heard sanitized versions. But not today. Today, it's untreated sewage:

"The little asshole of a principal won't change teachers; she's got them waving hand signals for certain responses; she won't call on him for any kind of response. Absolute silence in the classroom, no life forms tolerated; the first week of class she terrifies kids about state tests. Second grade for Christ sake. If Jake gets agitated, he's sent to the far side of the playground. She was shouting at us when we left today."

Out in the jungle, Jake can hear my angry tone, nothing new to him at home, but surprising out here. It's even possible that my rage on his behalf pleases him, because he's smiling under the jungle canopy.

"They've never had a kid in a wheelchair, of course, and don't want one. No one is friendly, teachers are paralyzed by the anal atmosphere; so are kids. It's like a maximum security prison, they line up in the cell block for the yard, guards patrol the perimeter looking for shivs."

What Jake makes of the comparison I have no idea, but one of Bill's novels is set in prison.

"His aide can't do anything?" he asks.

"She's as isolated as he is. Only the Special Ed teacher is kind. When things get too bad she lets him come to her class." Of course, Jake is not *in* her class because his parents, especially me, insisted that he be *mainstreamed*.

"The speech-language teacher from the county has never seen anything like this school. His teacher wouldn't let her into class. Never, in all her years, has she been forbidden to enter a class."

"Jake seems okay."

He does seem okay smiling in the jungle on this gloomy day, and I think we're talking about a fictional character in one of my stories, back when Bill was my teacher—smoking, as he is now on the pool steps, but wearing a tweed jacket and tie.

"Jake's more resilient that I am. Fortunately we have Thanksgiving break."

At least fortunate for Jake, who won't have a father angry at his misbehavior one minute, raging at the principal the next, turning his back on a shouting teacher the next. Thanksgiving will be a vacation for him. But for me, it begins the season of mandatory happiness, when my sister and I, feigning good cheer, scurried from one parent to the other, as Jake does now. Sans scurry. At this time of year, such memory patterns become neurological storms, and today's is a Category 5 hurricane.

Jake kicks his way out of the jungle, perhaps he's heard enough. But traveling on his back, he doesn't see the anaconda, aka pool sweep, lazily circling below him, and kicks right into its coils. I swim over to fight off the snake.

Bill asks, "So what happens now?"

"We'll call an IEP meeting and go to war. They're required to provide an *appropriate* education for him until he turns twenty-two. Not great, mind you, just *appropriate*. For a lot of parents we've known, things can get pretty ugly around that word."

Liberated from the anaconda, Jake kicks toward Bill, but the snake has squeezed something out of him. In the snake's coils is a huge turd. Jake tends toward constipation, a common complaint with these over-tight kids, and evidently, lying face up in warm water has relaxed him. It's quite a spectacular turd—a good two-day build-up, possibly three, and Bill, smoking and ruminating, hasn't noticed yet.

I make a quick decision, pluck a leathery philodendron leaf from the jungle, wrap the turd like a burrito, and holding it out of the water with one hand, sidestroke to the steps. I'm well used to handling shit, and the chlorinated pool will survive nicely.

"Sorry," I say. "I'll flush it down the toilet."

Bill is politely silent.

I walk naked into the house, where even the toilet is appalled. Water backs up ominously, and I'm pulling the lid off the tank to stop the flow when, abruptly, the turd passes and water recedes. Since the leaf is too big to flush, I rinse it like a diaper, follow my wet footprints back out the door, and return the leaf to the jungle.

When I slide back into the water, Jake is kicking around the pool and Bill is still sitting on the steps. There's a tactful silence. Nothing to do about the turd except forget it.

"You know what?" I ask.

Bill turns his head, and my tone makes Jake turn my way. Both of them wait.

"You know, Jake's mom lives in Menlo Park."

It's a fact of such stunning irrelevance that all of us, me included, can't imagine what's next.

"Just because *I* live in this district, there's no reason Jake has to go to Las Lomas." Except, of course, the one reason we're all tired of hearing about.

Two weeks later, at Laurel Elementary School, kids are fighting for a chance to push Jake's wheelchair, the principal and resource teacher take a special interest in him, so do office staff. His teacher is patient. The custodian jokes with him. My letters sent to the school board, superintendent and principal detailing Jake's treatment at Las Lomas are never answered. Why bother? They're happy he's gone and so are we. No more angry meetings, no lawyers.

Half a century later, the toilet of memory has flushed.

The Atomic Clock

ON THIS SPRING MORNING I'm closing the driveway gate—twelve feet of upright bars and ornamental steel hung from a single gatepost and latching outside the kitchen window with a house-shaking thump. But when I see Jake inside at the kitchen table, I stop the gate, causing it to vibrate at the sudden change of direction.

He's leaning forward in his new saddle chair, hamstrings stretched, boots on the floor, and what he's doing is reaching for a clock. Clocks are one of his obsessions. Calendars, spelling, buses, maps ... you never know what the next obsession will be. But right now it's clocks, and this is quite some clock. Digital of course, what isn't these days? After inserting a battery we'd been directed to wait up to thirty-six hours for the clock to contact a satellite and set the time. Jake has little patience for delay, and I was skeptical. But there it was: Pacific Standard Time! So accurate (less than one second deviation in three thousand years) that all other clocks are suspect, including the formerly authoritative clock on the microwave which is now, sometimes, out of sync with the new clock.

"Because," I say, "it's displaying the nearest minute while the atomic clock is calibrated to seconds."

As usual, explanations don't help, and he keeps twisting in his chair to check, and I am secretly pleased when they don't agree. *See, I told you so.*

The atomic clock also displays indoor and outdoor temperature to tenths of a degree, receiving transmissions from a remote unit outdoors. Pressing a switch will project time and temperature onto the ceiling. At night, Jake wants the clock in his bedroom in order to see the red numbers above his bed.

I once had a primitive sense of how things worked, could poke under the hood of a car, look inside a wristwatch and figure out the function of springs and cogs. I'd assembled a hi-fi from a kit. I could unscrew the mouthpiece off an old Ma Bell phone and imagine how the diaphragm translated voice to a small electric current wriggling through a line to another earpiece, the way a cord stretched between tin cans worked as a kid. Things made a kind of sense. But now, for $14.95 at Walgreen's, this little clock is talking to satellites and sensors and projecting digital readouts onto the ceiling.

Over a massive and crude kitchen table made from recycled lumber and scarred by nails, he's trying to pull the clock toward him. Which means transferring his desire for the clock through his compromised body, and that's no easy task. The strap around his chest keeps him from pitching face down on the table, but his body doesn't always know that, or trust it.

Since his hands turn the wrong way, he has to nudge the clock with the back of his hand, and to do that without tipping it over seems impossible. The clock may be amazing, but it's very unstable. Still he succeeds, and now I see what he's up to. To project time and temperature on the ceiling, he will have to raise his hand above the clock, and that's almost impossible.

With the gate still quivering in my hand, I watch as he lunges and, somehow, drops the back of his hand onto the switch. Now he's hanging face down over the table, and I'm in nearly the same position hanging from the gate. When he twists his head toward the ceiling, I crane to see time and temperature. I can't but evidently he can because he stays in the position for awhile, near prone but looking up.

He's in a real pickle. How can he possibly get his hand off his beloved clock without tipping it over? He turns face down and leans left. So do I. His hand moves the same way. It flops onto the table. The clock remains standing.

He sits up smiling.

A stranger looking through the kitchen window might see a handsome boy sitting at a table and smiling at a clock. They might notice the elastic band around his chest, and think, wait a minute, what's that band for? Then, looking more closely, they would notice something funny about his posture, hard to put your finger on at first, something about the way he's holding his body, his hands.

His proud father, however, is yelling through the closed window, an old casement that doesn't close very securely: "That was amazing, Jake."

Startled, he looks out at me. *Dad, what are you doing out there?*

"I'm just closing the gate."

And finally, as I set out to do minutes earlier, I latch the gate and come inside.

"Amazing, Jake. That was simply amazing."

His expression reveals little. He was surprised and then amused to see me outside. Now he's pleased that I'm back in the kitchen. The praise is fine of course. But it doesn't take much for a crippled kid to evoke praise from well-meaning adults, especially his father.

He pushes himself back in the chair. Very businesslike. Ready for third grade.

The ceiling reads 7:45 and 31 seconds.

No ... 32 seconds ... 33 ... 34 ...

You could go crazy trying to keep up with seconds. At least the temperature is stable at 66.4 degrees Fahrenheit. I help him stand and walk toward the car, well pleased with himself. I can tell because he's using his happy steps, like Buster Keaton, and my size-fourteen sandals are having a hard time of it flapping behind him.

The Coming of Dog

SEVERAL YEARS BEFORE JAKE'S BIRTH, a large man in a wheelchair appeared in my fiction writing class accompanied by a service dog, a light-colored lab. He drove an adapted van to the college and was a real presence in my classes, which he took several semesters. Young students listened to his comments about their stories and read his stories with interest. We became friends over the years, and when I told him about Jake's cerebral palsy, he suggested an assistance dog. Jake didn't much care for dogs, but how could a boy not love a trained dog?

The wait list was long, and it wasn't until Jake was in third grade that we had to face what we'd gotten ourselves into: he and Mom and Dad would have to live together for two weeks of training. Only a dog could have done it, and that barely. Jake and I stayed in a dorm room where there were three beds, four if you included his futon on the concrete floor, but Mom preferred a motel. I wasn't wild about a dorm myself, and since Jake didn't sleep well away from home, no one in the vicinity slept well.

In the dining area he was often too tense to eat which was fine with me. We'd return to our dorm room where I shoveled in whatever food he could tolerate under the circumstances: spaghetti with tons of Parmesan, yogurt, Fig Newtons, gallons of whole milk, Goldfish, graham crackers, salt and vinegar potato chips. Anything with calories but rarely from the common dining area since, under the circumstances, a picky eater was even more picky. After dinner

I would take him around campus on his bike or into town. Anything to get out of a wheelchair and away from people and dogs.

In the first week, we parent facilitators learned about handling dogs which, it was emphasized, are pack animals. In our case that meant parents who could barely speak to one another must become pack leaders. And that meant taking no shit. A dog should never enter a room before the pack leader; a failure to sit, stand or stay must be immediately corrected by a sharp jerk on a choke-chain collar that, if necessary, had spikes. Dogs have a tough neck, we were assured. Certainly the prong collar did command the attention of disobedient dogs, and also remorse from over-sensitive pack leaders. Anger must be avoided because dogs are emotional animals and pick up the vibe. We had to correct them without emotion. That was our mantra. When dogs were obedient, however, a little positive emotion was fine.

We learned to walk with a dog, shoulder to knee, to command *heel, sit, stay.* We learned commands for a dog to pick up a fallen object, to open doors, and to stay as nearly invisible as possible in public. We learned to toilet dogs, a revelation to me since my country dogs, so far as I was aware, rarely shat. These dogs, however, did shit, and their excrement had to be bagged and disposed of at regular times, lest an evacuation occur on the floor of Target.

Since an assistance dog acts as another pair of hands for a person in a wheelchair, I needed to make my peace with wheelchairs. At home we rarely used one: we walked together, Jake sat in the saddle chair, rode his bike, sat in the front seat of the car. Now he was one wheelchair among many.

In the training room, dogs emerged from kennels on command, returned on command. In preparation for our departure, we purchased two kennels, were given leashes and grooming equipment, none of which a country dog would recognize. We learned the importance of regular grooming that, to my astonishment, included tooth-brushing and nail-clipping. We learned that weight must be rigorously controlled, which meant no snacks and no Hoovering. An assistance dog never, ever, ate anything from the floor. In training, we walked dogs across a floor littered with French fries, without so much as a sniff, lest they be corrected. When they lay under a table and fries were dropped under their nose, not a twitch.

We learned that an assistance dog, when working, must not be petted or otherwise addressed by strangers. What this would mean for future bike trips around town I found out later. Ordinary Frisbees were not to be thrown (hard on dog hips), expensive medication for fleas and heartworm must be administered without fail. Two years had gone into the selection and training of these dogs, only forty percent of whom made it to this point. They were working dogs, could be recalled at any time if rules were not followed. They were not, it was emphasized, *not* pet dogs.

Jake spent as much time as possible away from dogs and people, sitting in our dorm typing on his keyboard plugged into my laptop. On the fourth day we were assigned one of three dogs we had worked with. Still thinking country dogs, I figured bigger was better, but we were assigned the smallest Lab/Retriever mix, Beatrice. For a boy afraid of dogs, the wisdom of this choice soon became clear. She was the least rambunctious and most sensitive to his anti-dog vibe. She lay quietly at the foot of his futon when he went to bed, and then obediently entered her kennel for the night. During the day, she walked or sat beside his wheelchair requiring few corrections. The dreaded prong collar was seldom needed as his mom and I took turns commanding her to walk dutifully beside our son's wheelchair, into an elevator, into a mall, into a restaurant, into a grocery store.

For two weeks our non-nuclear family managed classes together, but on hot evenings, Jake and I escaped disability. We went to a carnival, which he tolerated so long as we stayed off rides. We went to neighboring towns, explored outdoor cafés, he on his bike and never in a wheelchair. We raided Burger King. Anything to avoid bonding with other participants. It was our way of getting through dog school, leaving Mom to represent the family in the dining hall. She got to know participants and caregivers, shared stories, remembered names, and stayed in touch over the years.

Was there a moment when Beatrice became my dog more than Jake's or his mom's? The pattern was clear before we knew it. After Bea came home, she couldn't go to school unless his aide had trained for two weeks, and since that wasn't feasible, she stayed with me during the school day. Since I was retired and inclined toward vigorous exercise, we took long walks in the hills. Her forlorn expression—can't we do *something*?—always got me out of the house. I took her to dog parks, let her off leash at the beach where she chased balls into the surf. People on the street, women usually, would stand transfixed. *What a beautiful dog*, they'd say, gazing longingly at Beatrice, and occasionally I let them pet her. Even the homeless would sometimes pet this beautiful and agreeable animal whose first months with a puppy-raiser had adapted her to the chaos of children and family. A calm dog was required. And Beatrice was calm, attentive, sensitive to personal space. A bit shy. I liked that. In dog parks she tended to sniff warily around hyperactive dogs, might allow herself a brief frolic, but would then drift off soberly. She was like me at her age, anxious to get away from happy and well-adjusted kids and back into the sagebrush where I could stare mournfully into the far distance of Nevada. She and I shared mournful.

She trotted beside Jake's bike, sat under café tables with her blue vest on, slept on his bed (at my house, not Mom's), but kept a proper distance from him. Except, sometimes, near dawn, when it was cold and she would lie against him, keeping them both warm.

So it came to pass that after two weeks of dog training, we drove our separate cars home with a stranger in the back of the van in her kennel, with food and water dishes, grooming equipment, a blue vest, leashes, flea and heartworm medicine, and proper certification allowing her into theaters, restaurants, stores. Beatrice the dog, whose presence would radiate through the life of friends and community. Oh, there they are again riding through town, shopping, hanging out at cafés, that old guy steering the bike while his son pedals. And that beautiful yellow dog!

Soon the kennels (one for each home of course) were given away. When Jake's tutors arrive, Beatrice knows their cars and goes wagging out to meet them. Although we'd been taught how to discipline a dog that barks at visitors, Beatrice rarely barks. In fact, she has a hard time when commanded to *speak* which, for a person trapped in a wheelchair and needing assistance, is useful to summon help. She has to work herself into a frenzy, say at the prospect of dinner, before, looking devilish, she'll bark on command. Once.

Even Jake likes her although you need to know them both to know that. Five years after her arrival, he lets her lick his feet after a shower, lick his hands after she's nuzzled treats from his fingers. But the relationship remains formal. She is finally allowed to go to school with him because Jake's teacher encourages her presence and his current aide is dog savvy. In a high school Special Ed classroom, the full curative power of dog is unleashed. Shy kids, kids fearful of dogs, kids who rarely speak—touch her and, it is reported, are changed by the contact. On hospital visits to Jake's friends, she creates a joyous commotion when Master Jake, graciously, allows patients and doctors to visit with her.

By the time my son is sixteen, and Beatrice, white-muzzled, is rapidly approaching my age, she has at last found her calling.

Bowling in the Dark

THE SIGN FOR MEL'S BOWL is so bleached and broken, the asphalt parking lot so wrinkled and weedy, the lone oak so scraggly, that I've passed for years without remembering it was still here, and when Jake's adaptive PE teacher suggests that he bowl for Special Olympics, I have to ask for directions. Mel's is still a huge, well-lit space, almost surreal. Smoking is no longer allowed, but the smell remains in memory, like soup stock, in which today's odors of popcorn, beer, moldy carpets, spilled drinks, and deodorizers are simmering. Banners announce family night, disco bowling, extreme bowling, and something called *bowling in the dark*.

As we enter, Beatrice striding dutifully beside Jake's wheelchair, I can see Special Olympics students clumped at the farthest lanes. Some are so close to able-bodied that you scarcely notice—there are so many gradations of disability, even within Jake, whose neurological impulses are revealed in surprising ways.

Of course, it would be easier for him to bowl from his wheelchair, but I'm still pushing mobility. So I stand him up and march him to our designated lane, leaving his fourth-grade aide with little to do but watch. Our lane has a special bowling ramp: two parallel pipes six inches apart and raised about two feet above the floor. A ball is placed between the pipes. With a slight touch it can be sent rolling over the edge onto a ramp where, according to a well-known formula that I almost remember, it will accelerate. I do remember that the bowling ball and a feather would reach the hardwood at the same time, in a vacuum, but at Mel's, air resistance, friction, and wiggling pipes screw things up.

When it's our turn, I stand Jake beside the ramp and exhort him to reach for the ball assigned to him. He does. The back of his hand touches the ball, his body tightens his arm, and he overcomes the ball's inertia (another formula I've forgotten). Very slowly the ball rolls over the edge and down the sloping ramp to the floor.

At launch, however, the pipes wriggle, making the ball's stately progress toward the pins uncertain. Bumpers installed for Special Olympics make gutter balls impossible so, unless the ball stops altogether, which so far has not happened, some pins will go down. Jake's ball wanders and Beatrice, enduring the harsh sounds of a bowling alley, watches anxiously as we wait for whatever Jake has set in motion to happen.

I watch other participants whose movements, even those most apparently normal, are unpredictable, violent. Spastic of course. When I was in high school and bowling at Mel's, the operative word was *spaz*. One boy slings the ball back and forth, like a pendulum, working himself up for the throw. He's small, the ball looks big and dangerous, and I'm alert lest it fly backwards. But he's a tough little bugger, this kid, swinging the ball back and forth for some time before letting it arc onto the lane (in a way that must displease management), and the ball ricochets from side to side, from one gutter to the next, like a billiard shot. I try to guess where it will strike the pins, and with his arms hanging at his side, the kid watches, too. No matter what happens to the pins, however, he will raise his hands in triumph, in the accepted mode of athletes on TV.

His face is hard to describe. The eyes are slanted, the skin smooth as if burned in some hideous accident, but I doubt that's the case. His face simply has no affect, perhaps made smooth by lack of cognition. Returning to his seat, staring straight ahead, he swerves slightly toward Jake and me in what I recognize is a swerve of recognition: Why, there they are! Again.

The next kid pitches the ball with both hands onto the alley where it meanders between bumpers toward the wooden pins that I've begun to admire. Who invented the bowling pin? It's amazing how some pins, apparently doomed by a perfect shot, will remain standing while some crappy shot ricocheting off a bumper takes them all down. The physics must be quite complex. And then there's the *sound*, hardwood on hardwood! Even blind you could enjoy the satisfying violence of that collision, so crisp and confused. Whatever bowling in the dark entails, it must be fun listening to that sound and wondering what's gone down.

In other Special Olympics lanes, high school boys throw with great energy, almost anger, excited by the exuberant collisions and their own freedom to be violent. In fact, one of their counselors bowls with his charges, flinging the ball with more force than necessary and exploding the pins like a suicide bomb. He used to bowl years ago, he says, but his wife got rid of his ball.

One girl in our lane and also using our ramp can walk, and from a distance she might pass for normal, except for a hesitancy in her gait. She's pretty, about Jake's age, and her name is Emma. There's no help for it, I've been teaching *Madame Bovary* for years, and think of Emma Bovary who was crippled by romantic love. With both hands, Emma pushes the ball hard enough that it moves down the alley with some clarity of intent. Everything, of course, depends on how the ramp is aimed and what wiggling will do at launch. At first I try to get the ramp just right because I want Jake to be the best ramp bowler. But I soon give up. The sole point is waiting for a collision.

The adaptive PE teacher who got us into this afternoon away from school (which I suspect is the main reason Jake wants to be here) will periodically announce Jake's score with the enthusiasm many people use for the disabled, and which seems to please the older high school kids. Praise jacks up their energy level and boisterousness. Jake, however, is unmoved. He stands beneath my hands in his stylish riding boots, neckerchief around his neck, little interested in where the ball is going, even when his aide calls out, "Way to go, Jake!" or I say, "It's looking good, Jake, oh, no, it's swerving. Oh, well, we'll get the spare."

He's more interested in what other people are doing, like Emma who can't talk either, and like him has some evasive head-twisting tendency. She looks away as if averting her eyes from the impending collision, even when her aide tells her to look at the ball going down the alley. Sometimes her aide will hold Emma's head in both her own hands, forcing her to look down the alley. When Emma is released, she turns her head away, evincing no emotion. Unlike the boy with no expression, it's obvious there's a mind at work in Emma, but no indication that she cares about what she's done.

Watching Emma avert her eyes, I recognize myself watching the world peripherally. There are so many reasons to avert your eyes. Avoiding failure of course. Also, if you look directly, you must acknowledge. And if you acknowledge, you must act decisively. Also if you look directly at another person, they may know what you're thinking. Not a good idea. Or perhaps worse, you may know what they are thinking. Also it is impolite to stare. Also it can get you in a fight. There are so many reasons to avert your eyes. Like driving for example. Peripheral vision is great for driving. You can see what's coming from all directions. A good way to negotiate a hazardous world, peripheral vision. Go, Emma!

The other person bowling in our lane is Kathleen, a high school sophomore who, clearly, will be confined to a wheelchair for life. Internal forces, the tremendous isometric struggle of muscle against muscle against skeleton has attenuated her body, made it frail and misshapen. Her neck twists to one side, head tilting up, eyes uncoordinated. Her arms remind me of a daddy longlegs trying to escape a bathtub. She makes sounds, when her lungs compress under strain. But despite all this, and the fact that she lacks clarity of gaze or any of the other facial cues that I treasure in Jake and which suggest intelligence, she radiates intelligence. She is a monumental presence, twisted in her chair, behind which stands her mother who says Kathleen is doing well in high school, even without the advantage of Jake's high tech equipment.

When I ask Beatrice to "visit" her, putting her front paws on Kathleen's lap, the light in the girl's face, the sounds she makes, are so emotional that I tear up and, like Emma, avert my eyes. Weeks from now Kathleen will be on the waiting list for her own companion dog. It's so clear that a dog will bring joy to her life.

Kathleen's mother wheels her daughter to the ramp. The girl strains forward from her wheelchair. Her face twists back over her shoulder, elbow and wrist joints move in impossible ways as her left hand reaches across her body to help her right hand reach for the ball.

It is an act of will I've seen in Olympic weight lifters, about to lift from the floor more weight than is humanly possible. Belt strapped around his waist, stooping to grasp the bar, neck tendons and muscles flaring as he lifts the bar off the floor, he either gets his body under the tremendous weight, extending it over his head, or fails and drops it to the mat. Her hand curves backward against the struggle in her own body, focused will against impossibility, spindly arm twisting her palm under the ball. Then, with a convulsion of her entire body, she launches the ball with more force than Jake will ever muster. What Kathleen has just accomplished defies comprehension. The ball moves down the lane with some alacrity, as if really headed someplace, and Kathleen watches obliquely. Pins fall.

When we prepare to leave, the boy with no expression approaches with his aide. She asks him to repeat what he has said. He mumbles. I lean down but can't make out his words, smooshed together in a way I would love to hear from Jake.

The aide translates: *I like your dog.* She tells him to wish us a happy Thanksgiving, and this time, forewarned, I do understand. I ask Jake to respond with a wave. He thinks about it for awhile, long enough to be rude, before flicking a minimal wave that most people wouldn't recognize as a wave. He's just learning the etiquette of mandatory courtesy, and this reluctant wave is a major concession, but a long way from his finest full-body wave, both arms splayed in the air, ear-to-ear smile, body rigid.

Beatrice's tail is up and wagging because we're going to escape this house of violence and confusion. She's got light in her eye, is looking quite alert and noble in her blue vest, a working dog standing beside her master in his wheelchair, ready to go. And we do—Jake, his aide, his father, and Beatrice—out through a door I first entered fifty years ago.

The Story Writer

SUNDAY DINNER HAS PASSED amiably enough, shoveling fork loads of pasta into Jake's mouth, followed by wads of garlicky salad and chunks of sourdough bread soaked in salad bowl leavings: lemon, olive oil, garlic, feta, tomato. He's drinking Pear Collage through a straw, I'm on my second beer, and we're both anointed with spaghetti sauce, rogue bread crumbs and lettuce scraps. Beatrice is doing clean up.

Since it's time for fourth-grade spelling homework, I march him into the bedroom and see that his riding boots, the ideal walking boots these past months, are now rolling inward under the pressure of his tight and increasingly powerful muscles. As a result his feet are splaying out. *Pronation* is our latest worry, and I'm thinking about orthotics or another surgery. I settle him at his desk, a piece of plywood suspended from the wall, Beatrice lies down at his feet, and I lie down on his bed, my perk on spelling night.

He's a good speller (especially if I exaggerate consonants, warn of silent e's, caution about weird English spellings) and a good phonetic speller of words he doesn't know. And now, since the qwerty keyboard has been a great success, we've even begun to converse using separate keyboards. He'll read my questions on screen and type single word answers, sometimes two or three words if pushed. We call them chats.

Now, pleased with our progress these past months, I'm admiring his posture in the saddle chair, erect, boots on the floor, as he glances over, waiting for the first word. Maybe it's my second beer, but for a moment I'm not in his bedroom but back in a college writing class.

I stand up, no small matter after spaghetti, beer and salad, and sit down beside him. "I've got an idea, Jake."

He gives me his wary expression: *Is this something educational?*

"How about writing a story tonight instead of spelling?"

My mantra for beginning writers was *Just start writing and the rest will come,* but Jake's not given to writing without a prompt. The free flow of written language is not his thing.

"Tell you what. What if we write together?"

He opens his mouth in cautious agreement.

So I open my mouth: "Well …" I say, with no idea what I am going to say, "what we need for a story is …" What? What *is* necessary for a story? Have I ever satisfactorily answered that question?

"What we need … are … characters."

He looks at me.

"You got a character in mind?"

His response is instant. Stretching his fingers through the holes of the plastic key guard, he spells one of his current, obsessive words: *penney.*

"Who's Penney?"

Tiger he types immediately.

He loves to look at and talk about African animals on calendars, but this is my first inkling of Penney's identity, and his quick response triggers my own: "So *where* is this Penney tiger?"

How many thousands of times have I asked a student for more detail?

Zoo he types. Now on the screen are three words: *Penney tiger zoo.*

"Okay … Jake …" I'm tearing up and have to pause for surreptitious eye wipe. "Okay … now … just *how* did Penney get into the zoo?"

He delivers a quizzical look. Translation: *What do you mean? If the tiger is in the zoo, who cares how it got there?*

Too late, the weepy-eyed English teacher is thinking verbs, and no wimpy verbs, we want energetic verbs.

I move the cursor back in front of *zoo*. "How about a verb?"

He knows verbs from school and from our spelling, but he's still wary: *What the hell is going on? We were having fun and now it's gotten like school?*

"How about *walk, climb?*"

He makes his scrunched up negative face.

"How about *dash, creep, jump?*"

No dice.

Reluctantly, I offer the flaccid verb I've been avoiding: "*Go?*"

His face comes alive and he types: *Penney tiger goes zoo.* I am pleased to note that verb and subject agree, but now we're up against the preposition, a constant problem for second-language students. Which, I suppose, Jake is.

"*Into* the zoo? *In* the zoo? *Around* the zoo? *To* the zoo."

As expected, prepositions are of no interest and he lets me know it with a stiff body and whine. I wait. Finally, with considerable irritation, he types *to*, which brings us to the article. He's still whining and I'm afraid to lose the moment. On the other hand, goddamn it, he knows what article is necessary, he just doesn't want to do it.

"Tell you what, you type the first letter, I'll type the next."

He goes for that and types *t*.

I type *h*.

He types *e*.

And so it comes to pass that *Penney tiger goes to the zoo.* I'm so moved that I have to pause and swallow a sniffle.

"Is it a sentence?"

No problem. He leans back in the saddle, leverages a finger through the key guard and stabs a period, causing the disembodied computer voice to intone: *Penney tiger goes to the zoo.*

His face lights up and my sniffle edges toward blubber. "Okay now, Jake ... so ... Penney's at the zoo. Now what happens?"

Instant response: *Elephant*.

"Got a verb?"

No response.

"*Walk, run, sit, stand*?"

Negative.

"Or ..." this is a story after all, "does elephant say something?"

Instant response. He rears back, punches out *says*.

"What does elephant say?"

Fart.

"To whom is elephant speaking?" He gives me a look. *Whom?* The objective pronoun does sound weird these days, but I can't help it, I'm in full teacher mode.

No response.

"To Penney?"

Jake opens his mouth wide—*yes*—and even volunteers the preposition: *to Penney*.

Now, too late, I notice that the keyboard template he's using (one of several) lacks quotation marks. What are we going to do about a talking elephant? I move the cursor in front of *fart*. "How about a comma to suggest that elephant is speaking?"

He stabs a comma. I move the cursor after *fart* and suggest, drolly it seems to me, that a fart might be exclamatory. He knows about exclamation marks but in this case, blatantly, ignores the advice and stabs a question mark.

The poor computer, unable to decide if elephant is commanding a fart or asking who's responsible, does it's best to sound quizzical: *Elephant says to Penney, fart?*

We both laugh.

"So now what happens?"

What happens is that a speechless boy likes simple sentences, dialog without quotation marks, and present tense—a writer in the modern mode:

Penney tiger goes to the zoo. Elephant says to Penney, fart? Penney says to elephant, yo. Zebra eats Penney's food. Eagle flies in and farts on Penney.

Over the next days his stories come faster than any I've written over the years. *Hippo and elephant are in the zoo when yak farts! Then eagle says, farts? And then eagle falls on his head? And his feet stick up in the air and he farts?*

Surprising characters appear: armadillo, gorilla, orangutan. All correctly spelled. One of his stories is hung over the desk in his resource room. Teachers read his stories and laugh. And then one day he leaves the actual fart to the reader's imagination, a technique I'd taught for years. Let your reader do the work.

An elephant named JW swam to the zoo on the island with a cat on his head where a fox said, Smell this you big dumb cat?

The next day: *Rat sneaks into the zoo. Elephant sees rat. Eagle smells stink? Rat looks at elephant.*

Is rat giving elephant an accusatory look, a guilt trip? Or is eagle stirring up trouble by imagining a stink? The question mark complicates matters. Or is rat, the actual farter, trying to throw eagle off the track by casting blame on elephant, a tactic not unknown in farty classrooms. On the other hand, sneaky rat may be casting his lot with eagle against elephant, the one dependable character in the story.

I doubt any of these possibilities are conscious with Jake, which is just as well, because writers should keep their mouths shut. Certainly, this writer isn't talking. And this reader can't. He's blubbering.

Which causes the writer to look up?

The Outcast

IT'S YET ANOTHER FIELD TRIP, this one for Jake's fifth-grade class, and I'm wondering when field trips became de rigueur. In my day we stayed at school, variously bored or apprehensive, all day, every day. Arriving from the sagebrush outside Reno, I'd wander around in the general vicinity of kids who seemed to know one another, waiting for class where I could vanish. A school bus would be even worse because kids who knew one another saved seats and only an outcast sat alone. I hated buses.

Jake, however, loves buses, often the highpoint of a field trip. But they're rarely equipped for wheelchairs, and rather than make a big assertive stink about the need for an accessible bus, I hoist him aboard to sit beside his aide, while I drive our van and wheelchair to meet them at the other end. Everybody on the bus knows Jake. They're used to him, even seem to like him.

On the last field trip he'd sailed on an authentic Spanish galleon that did not in any way conform to the Americans with Disabilities Act of 1990. If it had, you wouldn't have a galleon any longer. The whole point of the Columbus experience was treacherous decks and cramped quarters, huge clumsy sails which kids, with a good deal of *yo-ho-hoing*, could help raise while coiling and uncoiling rope and using belaying pins, all the while scrambling along narrow gangways or down a steep ladder into a cabin where the old maps were spread out, where navigation and compasses were discussed, and where some would grow listless and turn a bilious green.

A wheelchair was out of the question, but so was walking in our usual manner because a galleon was all angles, slopes, coils, lines, booms, masts, steps and tangles of kids. The ship's crew, alarmed at the spectacle of a crippled boy and his father moving about their vessel, were obviously wondering how such a situation had ever been allowed in the first place. Which made me even more determined that Jake should have the full galleon experience. Since his aide couldn't do it, I carried or half-walked him from one demonstration to the next.

Photographs taken by his aide reveal a boy not particularly happy with his educational experience. Except for one series of photos, when students got to steer the galleon from a wheel perched high enough off the deck for the steersman to see over the bow, sort of like a sea-going podium. Naturally, I insisted Jake have a turn. To the alarm of the captain and mate, I hoisted him up to the podium, big drop-offs on all sides, the boat rocking, a kid who could barely stand much less hold on and an old guy—it had disaster written all over it. Insurance claims. Suits. The loss of the galleon.

But it was too late. I stood behind him while he tried to grab the wheel spokes with hands that rotate away from the grasping position normal to humans and monkeys, even squirrels and possums. So I reached around his shoulders helping him steer to starboard or port as called by the apprehensive mate. Classmates stood below watching him bring the galleon toward the dock. It's the only time Jake smiled the entire trip, and those photographs would light a darkened room. Call it education if you must.

This year's fifth-grade field trip is aboard a marine research vessel that does accommodate wheelchairs, which is good news since I need to stop carrying him. He's heavier, I'm older. But I can still lift him into the front seat, load the wheelchair up a portable ramp, unload at the harbor, get him buckled into the chair and roll him across a gangplank onto the deck of the research vessel and into the classroom amidships. Last year on the galleon, it was cold on the bay. This year on a modern vessel, it's warm and stuffy in the classroom. His aide is not with us today, so Jake didn't ride the bus.

Once we're on the bay, I wheel him on deck to watch classmates scoop plankton samples from the dingy water, wheel him back to the classroom where the plankton is magnified on a TV monitor. To my surprise, these creatures at the bottom of the food chain have an assortment of tentacles, misplaced eyes, creepy looking bodies, if you can call them bodies, all of which they sacrifice for the rest of us. The basic message of this day is pretty clear—big stuff eats little stuff.

"And then you eat a fish sandwich at Burger King," I say.

Jake's not impressed with educational whimsy, nor is he much interested in watching students match what is on the screen with pictures from a chart. We go back on deck for seawater samples. We go back inside for calculations of salinity and temperature, and information about effects of rainfall and sunlight. I'm surprised at the seasonal variations of salinity and how shallow the San Francisco Bay is. We go back on deck for mud dredged from the bottom, including worms and their casings and all the other stuff that descends into mud. Kids are encouraged to smear mud on their faces, as an initiation into the brotherhood of the bay. Mud is brought for Jake to touch and for his father to smear on his son's face. With mud around their eyes, on their foreheads, cheeks, arms, the class looks like a football team. Or soldiers in Iraq.

Next his fellow students haul in a net with squiggly things in it, including a stingray and small fish that provide evidence the food chain is working. Jake perks up at the appearance of actual fish. Also the ray is making a dramatic commotion in its trough of seawater. A biologist removes the stinger so the kids can touch the ray. Not to worry, he says, they grow back. Like a fingernail.

So far so good. But four hours on the bay is about an hour too much watching other people do things. When we return to the classroom for a game of Jeopardy employing newly learned biological concepts, Jake begins to complain. He wants off the boat. I explain that we're stuck.

"We'll be in the harbor soon."

Not soon enough. His cries begin to disturb Jeopardy, so I wheel him back on deck where the ray is still flopping about in its trough of seawater. The harbor is approaching, the same harbor into which he had steered the galleon, but today the tide is very low, and now that I've learned how shallow the bay is, I'm surprised we're still afloat.

"Look at the mudflats, Jake. It's a very low tide."

Since he touched mud and has some smeared below each eye and on his nose, I figure mud-talk may prevent a total breakdown of the sort that will make him, quite literally, an outcast.

"But these tides are pretty wimpy," I say. "Now up in Alaska with twenty-foot tides, now those were mudflats. Our skiff would get stranded way out …"

He's not buying diversion: *I want off. Now.* He's screaming, but the ship's engines are reversing near the dock, and it looks as if we're going to escape before a full screaming breakdown. So I relax. But not for long. The pier, which was level with the deck when we came aboard, is now far above us.

"How can we get off?" I ask a deck hand.

"Can you wait for the class picture?" he asks.

Jake screams. Delays will not be tolerated, and we both know that a crowd of classmates will make things worse.

"I think he needs to get off."

The steel gangway we had crossed onto the ship won't reach down to the deck now, a common problem for the crew, I suppose, but less common with a screaming boy in a wheelchair and an agitated father. Two young men, college students I'd guess, drag over the storage chest that holds life vests. His vest is removed and put inside. Someone on the dock lowers the gangway at a steep angle to the top of the chest. A crewmember brings a small crate as a step up.

"Should we carry him up in the wheelchair?" a voice asks.

That seems dangerous to me. Also, of course, I'm reluctant to accept help, even though age should be making it more acceptable. And I'd toted him all over the galleon last year, so a few steps up a gangway should be no problem.

"I'll take him up," I say. "Then you can bring the chair."

I stand him from the chair, lift him under my left arm as I've done for years, but not recently. He's screaming and crew members are watching with alarm as I step up onto the locker. The jagged steel mesh of the gangway looks like good footing, and I calculate six or seven steps will get us to the dock. I can use my right hand on the railing to help pull us up (a combined weight of two-hundred-sixty pounds, I figure, more like two-seventy since after Christmas, I'm pretty porky).

I take my first step.

"Look out, it's slippery," a voice calls.

The jagged mesh doesn't look slippery, but simultaneous with the warning my right foot, or rather the sports sandal on my foot, slips, and we begin to fall face first. I let go of the railing, straight arm the gangway and do break our fall. However, Jake's head continues forward, and his face hits the jagged metal.

There is stunned silence. Deckhands drag him up the ramp and I follow. Band-Aids and ice appear, but he'll have nothing to do with such nostrums. His sole occupation is crying. His abraded nose does not appear to be broken, and his forehead scrape seems minor. A concussion seems unlikely.

His wheelchair appears on the dock, and his rigid body is folded into it. One side of his nose looks like grated cheese, but he seems okay. He has a high pain threshold and seems to be crying more from outrage than pain. Students gathered below for their class photo stare up at their fallen classmate. Crew members look shaken. And for a moment I'm back in grade school, the pathetic kid with a bloody knee ringed by concern. Jake, however, is not pathetic. He's pissed and letting everyone know it as I wipe his face with a towel, dab the bloody striations on his nose which aren't deep. The forehead scrape is bruising slightly.

A woman from the harbor office, very concerned, appears and I assure her that we're fine, not to worry, and I sign a piece of paper. He's calming down. He's fallen from chairs. Fallen face down at school on a hardwood floor and not broken any teeth or his nose, or been knocked-out or concussed. He fell off an x-ray table. Generally he finds bruises and scrapes, *dings* in our parlance, amusing. Now back in the car and offered a salt and vinegar chip, he begins to forget to cry, and I begin my interrogation.

No, my nose isn't sore when you wiggle it.

Yes, the field trip was fine.

Yes, I might go on the bay again.

Yes, I want to go to school tomorrow.

"You're a tough kid."

Whatever. Just keep the chips coming.

Next day, he does go to school with a swollen nose and slightly bruised forehead. I check on him later in the morning, arriving into the chaos of a grade school recess. He's easy to find because his wheelchair provides a still point around which kids are running, screaming, banging into one another. Friendship clusters are forming and dispersing, or hanging together for some important business. Balls carom off backboards. And yes, a few loners are watching.

Jake is not one of them. He and his aide are right in the middle of the melee, and he's as wired as any of the other kids, legs extended in a really crappy posture that needs to be addressed with his aide, arms extended, fingers stretched to his adaptive communication device attached to his chair. Whatever he's typing can't be heard in all the noise or read in the bright light. But that doesn't seem to bother him. He's punching keys, laughing.

No one, kids or teachers, notices an old man standing at the edge of the playground. And that's just as well because, after sixty-eight years, I want to be alone in this moment. Savoring it.

Ten Thousand Steps

I'M WALKING TO JAKE'S new middle school in light rain, doing what I swore not to do after the Las Lomas disaster: anticipating his future. In this case, plotting a route for his power wheelchair that he can steer with his head. Practicing at the shopping center, I would follow him with a remote stop switch.

"Stop, Jake, wait for those people. Let them pass, they don't expect you to turn suddenly."

If he looks left, the chair turns that way. If he freezes up at a near collision, his head rears back and the chair powers forward rather than stopping. To stop, he needs to move his head forward off the switch in the headrest, but at times of danger or confusion his body instinctively pushes back.

There's much to learn about driving a power chair with your head. For both of us. Also for Beatrice who, leashed to the chair, is confused by sudden changes of direction. So I've taken to leaving her home, and since Jake's mom is also daunted by hazards of the chair, I'm sole wheelchair guide. And now I'm plotting a route to school.

This morning's paper announced a new fitness goal: ten thousand steps, any old steps, just take them. Just reading the article gave me a good start. After looking for my reading glasses, and by the time Beatrice had peed twice, pooped once, and I'd watered the garden, and found the glasses but misplaced the paper, I was well on my way to fitness. And that was twelve hours ago.

Now I'm headed into bonus territory, leaving Jake at home with a caregiver.

The multi-purpose room is packed with folding chairs and parents sitting attentively and listening to a speaker. There are vacant seats high in the bleachers, but I decide to stand. It's my preferred mode, tentative, ready to escape. Jake doesn't like crowds either, but he doesn't need to sneak away or hide—he can scream.

The speaker strains against the lousy acoustics in this cavernous room. Raised basketball standards and bleachers signal organized sports. In my day there was no multi-purpose room, much less a middle school. I'm standing in a foreign country.

This speaker, I will discover, is vice principal of the school. She's introducing a video produced by the students themselves. This middle school has a full video production facility where students prepare daily news broadcasts. Of course, it would. This school ranks among the best in the state, and competition for college is ferocious. I think I see on the gathered faces a kind of aggressive anxiety.

In Jake's last years at elementary school, I met few parents, but some of their kids had walked around town with us, Jake on his bike, me steering on one side, Beatrice walking dutifully on the other side. As time passed, we saw them and their parents at intersections, and we waved. Some of those parents, and no doubt others in this multi-purpose room, will know about the kid in a wheelchair with a speaking device, the kid who sometimes has to leave class for a surreptitious diaper change or because he's disruptive, a kid excused from assemblies he can't abide. Like his father.

In the video, kids are playing basketball and soccer. We are told there are appropriate changing rooms, and with no frame of reference but high school, I imagine snapping towels, guys with circumcised dicks, the smell of jockstraps, the ripening odors of maturity and fear, and me poised for escape. But this is middle school. Just relax! Of course that was my advice to myself trying to pee at high school urinals, and about as helpful then as now. Students on the video talk about advanced classes and electives, lacrosse and tennis, and school lockers. Lockers! I hear them slamming down the long gauntlet of high school corridors. Just relax.

The next speaker, an imposing white-haired man, has served as principal longer than any other in the area. He suggests, diplomatically, that parents might want to ease off after-school activities—all those academic preparation programs, music lessons, sports, ballet.

"Fifteen years ago," he says, "it was a different world. Kids had more time to themselves. There was less pressure. This will be a big transition year and they will need some space."

Fifteen years ago, Bub? Try fifty.

The PTA president, an energetic young woman I must have seen around town, solicits parent volunteers, and for a moment I'm tempted. PTA is huge in this area, run by energetic professional women, and this would be a chance for me to give something back to the school. But I'm in full regression, arranging my face in a way that suggests, really, I'd love to stay but urgent business is calling me away. I do have a valid excuse, Jake's caregiver must leave, but I'm really fleeing letterman sweaters and class presidents.

At middle school!

By the time I get home I'm well over ten thousand steps and expecting to find Jake and his caregiver at the computer, Beatrice under the table. I'm annoyed to find them playing with Jake's old farm puzzle. Regression annoys me. Beatrice does manage to stand on my arrival, then changes her mind and lies down again.

"Well," I say, taking off my wet jacket, "that's some school you're going to, Jake."

In his current fifth-grade class kids are tolerant and affectionate toward him, he's well-known and well-liked thanks to an aide who cares for him as one of her own children. But in four months, a new and as yet unhired aide will be wheeling him from class to class through a minefield of hormones and academic pressure.

"It'll be quite a change," I say, echoing the principal's warning and my own fears.

But what, really, will change for Jake? There'll be a new aide, and multiple teachers instead of one. He'll know many of the kids. He's accustomed to a wheelchair and diapers even if his father is not. The academic heat will be intense, but he'll have assistance, and he can always escape by disrupting class. And adolescence? Well, what of it? Likely to be more awkward for me than him. His computer already speaks with a man's voice, and about the logistical problems of masturbation? That's easy. I don't think about it. Who's worried about change?

Jake's caregiver for one. Over-staying his visa during a time of terror has proven serious business, and he must soon return to Brazil. After he leaves, I walk Jake into his room, strip off his clothes, a process becoming more difficult as he grows stronger, more resistant and rigid. I'm the last one still attempting to toilet him, but can't face the struggle tonight. Easier to change a diaper. And five more steps is nothing to be sneezed at.

A New Sheriff in Town

AT THE END OF A SCHOOL DAY, there is surely no country in the world with a scene such as this: two-ton SUVs dwarfing their drivers, mothers mostly, lined up in front of school and blocking the entrance to handicapped parking. Righteously annoyed, I enter through the exit. I mean, officer, my son's handicapped, has a wheelchair, can't talk, uses adaptive equipment, and those goddamned SUVs are illegally parked. How's a fellow supposed to reach handicapped parking?

Once parked and with time to kill, I decide to check my blood pressure as recommended by my cardiologist. It's a recent obsession, as throwing the *I Ching* was at one point in my life, and these readings are about as enigmatic. Keeping my arm out of sight like a masturbating teenager, I pump up and discover that I'm 40 points higher than this morning. Let's say ten points for those goddamned SUVs. That leaves thirty points for Jake's behavior.

Transition from elementary to middle school has been tough for all of us, although what Jake thinks is a mystery. He'll answer yes/no questions the way I took tests in high school: give them what they want. He says he's fine with middle school life, but I think his blood pressure must be up, too, because he's more disruptive in class and has been sent to the principal's office in the company of his new aide, who's had a lot to learn in three weeks: how to read Jake's expressions and translate his thoughts, help him do assignments, find ways for him to participate, and also change a diaper. He must not have a criminal record and must have at least an eighth-grade education. And around here, where babysitters make more than aides, there aren't a lot of applicants for the position of inclusion aide.

Last year, Jake's aide mothered him through elementary school, made sure he had friends, that teachers saw him as bright and capable, and teased him out of behavioral issues. When she became pregnant, however, her doctor said she couldn't lift a handicapped kid from a wheelchair.

The end-of-school buzzer goes off. I hide the blood pressure cuff under the seat as middle-schoolers begin swarming past the van, some sprouting breasts, the boys facial hair suggesting that soon, if not already, they'll be colliding in the sticky scrums of sex. A couple of days ago Jake typed *boner* on his computer and touched his left eye, meaning *I don't know*. His aide last year hadn't been allowed to attend the boys-only sex-ed session, so I was unclear about specifics. And didn't press for details. Drawings showed genitalia at various ages, but no boners. Perhaps that's been left to middle school.

"It's slang," I told him. "For an erection."

As usual, Beatrice comes with me to Jake's classroom, one of the portables way out by the soccer field, and we see him headed our way (out early, that's alarming). He's being pushed by his new aide, a man in his fifties, almost military in bearing, and not in the least maternal. He's so muscular and fit that I feel intimidated. Why can't I look like that? Ice hockey had been his sport. Now he umpires Little League baseball. He never mentions children of his own and says he got into caregiving for his wife's mother with Alzheimer's.

"That can be a terrible burden," I'd said.

He looked at me sharply, straight in the eye, almost challenging. "Why would it be?"

Why would a mother-in-law with Alzheimer's be a burden? I was too surprised to answer.

"How could caring for a loved one be a burden?"

I'd never heard the term *loved one* used with such authority.

Now my own loved one is coming toward me in a wheelchair pushed by an ex-hockey player, a man who is, emphatically, not a surrogate mother, who sternly insists that you pay attention in class, not be disruptive, use your communication equipment and read assignments. When I ask Jake how his day went, holding out my hands, left *bad*, right *good*, he always taps *good*. I don't press the issue, but out of his hearing, his aide often tells me it was a bad day.

So far Jake's performance has been excused by the trauma of transition, but last night we had a chat at our two keyboards. I typed: "Can I ask your aide if you had a good day tomorrow?"

Jake typed *yes.*

"And if he says it's a good day, we go to the café after school?"

Yes.

"And if he says it's a bad day, we come home?"

Yes.

I felt like a lawyer drawing up a contract. At morning drop off, I repeated our agreement, and now comes the moment of truth, like one of those old westerns where the least hesitation or doubt would get you killed. Since doubt is my mother's milk, I'd have been face down in the dusty street, riddled with bullets.

If Jake has had a bad day, he can't ride his bike to the café to watch trains and buses and drink milk and eat salt and vinegar potato chips. His face will collapse in despair, and I'll question everything we're doing. Are we regressing to the bad old days at Las Lomas when, because of my own failings, I punished him? Should I, as punishment now, deny him exercise after a long day in a wheelchair? Is his new aide himself part of the problem? Or, worst doubt of all, are regular classes the problem? Maybe he *should* be in Special Ed. For the rest of his life.

So I'm face down in the dusty street.

Jake, however, is sitting upright in his wheelchair in the manner approved by teachers and Gary Cooper. Look me in the eye, pardner, not easy for him to do at the best of times. That he's doing so now could be a hopeful sign, unless it's defiance: *Let's get it over with. I messed up again.*

But he's also smiling. Which is good. Unless that, too, is defiant: *What are you going to do to a kid in a wheelchair, Dad? Huh?*

On the other hand his posture and smile may well mean what I hope they mean: *I did it, Dad. Now I get to hang out at the café and ride El Camino.*

The distance between us diminishes according to an equation that, at his age, I might have been able to solve. If a boy in a wheelchair is being pushed at a more or less steady rate, say two miles an hour, toward his father who is approaching at what might be called an amble (feigning nonchalance), and the initial distance between them is two hundred feet, how soon and where will they meet?

His aide looks enigmatic. He could be suppressing a grin, but his carriage and manner are so much that of a professional umpire, or sheriff, that I can't read him.

We stop about five feet apart for dramatic effect. Since I've gotten us into this confrontation, I have no choice but to step forward.

"How'd it go today?" I ask holding out closed fists.

Jake quickly taps my right hand, *good.*

"Can I ask Tony?"

Jake opens his mouth. *Yes.*

Behind him, his aide's tight expression opens into a smile, and I feel twenty, forty, sixty millimeters of mercury rush from my body.

"He had a great day!"

I reach for Jake's hand, shake it. "Way to go, dude."

Rigid with delight, he's straining at his wheelchair straps, and Beatrice is wriggling and wagging beside him, little knowing that her own fate had hung in the balance. An afternoon at home is not her idea of fun.

But now with his dog on one side, me on the other, and his aide pushing, Jake and his posse ride toward town, heads high on this splendid September afternoon.

Betty

WE'RE SITTING SIDE BY SIDE at the kitchen table, Jake's adaptive keyboard plugged into my laptop, our chat appearing on its screen. He's slow, deliberate, favoring abbreviations or single words, while I type fast making lots of errors. We're discussing Betty, widow of my colleague and mentor at the college. He was a bombardier over Italy and Germany when cigarettes were part of the game, and he survived the war but fifty years later cigarettes killed him. Craggy and boyish right to the end, smoking a pipe by then, leather patches on his tweed jacket, he was a man for whom moral ambiguity simply did not exist. He allowed no self-deception, no compromise. He set a standard I rarely met, and even now, seven years after his death, I'm still asking myself, *What would Mel do?* And then wincing at the answer.

Jake has come to love his widow, Betty. When we visit, he sits with her on her white couch, and I sit opposite in the chair favored by the dead man, where I took a snapshot of the seventy-eight-year-old widow and twelve-year-old boy leaning together like lovers, reading a book, faces lit by happiness so rare in her infirmity. The photograph makes people smile. They can't believe it's the same woman.

But she died early this morning, and Jake was still asleep when I got the call. Now I type: "Our plans for visiting Betty have changed."

His body stiffens. He doesn't like plans to change.

"Something has happened."

He knows death. My colleague Linda, our good friend, died of cancer three years ago, and in the tradition of Buddhists had lain unembalmed for three days, morphing into something ghastly. Her godchild, about Jake's age, tried to look at the remains of his godmother, averting his eyes before fleeing the room. Later he sat with us before her corpse, and I admired his courage. Jake saw only her ashes dispersed on a wind-scoured knoll at seven-thousand feet in the Sierra, leaning against my knees as we talked about the dead woman, read poems, and made a circle of stones for her ashes.

Now I type: "I got a phone call."

He reads, waits.

"You know that convalescent hospital, where we last saw Betty?"

Of course he knows the hospital. That's where we're going to visit her day after tomorrow.

He reads and types: *y*, his abbreviation for yes.

I can hear Betty's long-dead husband Mel saying: What are you avoiding? If he was old enough for Linda, he's certainly old enough for my wife.

I type: "Betty died last night."

Jake's body grows rigid, arms extending in his neurological version of rigor mortis for the living.

"Remember Linda three years ago?"

I don't know what he remembers of our ceremony for Linda. What I remember most vividly is walking him through windy sage on a nondescript hill above Indian Valley, and his weight against my knees as we sit and watch her ashes and bone fragments fall onto sandy rubble.

Now he's too tense to type, so he opens his mouth, meaning *yes*. Yes, he remembers Linda's death. But that knowing had come slowly. This time it's pure shock. He's rigid.

"Friends are meeting at Betty's house," I type. "Do you want to go? It'll be crowded."

His body is stone hard, legs and arms extended, grimacing with tension. He doesn't like big gatherings—school assemblies, birthday parties, concerts—and I'm confident he won't want to go.

He reaches for the keyboard. A single letter appears on the computer screen. *Y.*

"You're sure?"

Y.

I consider logistics and type: "Should we go early ahead of the crowd?"

Y.

"Shall we take that photograph of you and Betty on the couch?"

Y.

So Sunday before Christmas, about an hour before the memorial begins, we stand at her door as we used to do, waiting for her to open it, leaning on a cane or walker. Later, at the convalescent hospital, I would walk Jake to her bed, passing other old people waiting to die. Some smiled at us, as if we had come to visit them.

A woman opens the door. It is Betty's daughter from Chicago.

"So this is Jake," she says. "I've heard so much about you."

Jake is not looking at her. He's searching for Betty or her son, so familiar from these past years living with his mother, and we see him inside laying out refreshments on a table. Her other son, thirty miles away, no longer spoke to his mother and, we are now informed, won't be here today. I can't believe it. Betty could be tough and acerbic, but what must Jake think about a son who won't attend his mother's memorial?

He's so tight I can barely move him over the threshold into the hallway where Betty would have led our ritual tour of the house. He never tired of the tour, studying photographs and memorabilia of her married life, looking for any change since his last visit.

"Jake loved your mom's house," I tell Betty's daughter. "Can we make a final tour?"

"Of course," she says, "Are you okay on your own?"

"Oh, yes. He's memorized every detail of this house."

We follow a line of masking tape on the floor. When her sight failed, the tape helped Betty find her way through the house on her walker. "Like following bread crumbs through the forest with an emergency beeper pinned to my shirt," she'd joked. Even at the end she was droll. Humor had kept her going until the third fall sent her to the convalescent hospital.

Through the kitchen, bath, her bedroom, Jake searches for any shift of position in photos, bottles, artifacts of widowhood. Stiffly, he follows the masking tape back to the living room where the white couch has been moved. Shock turns him into a statue, and we stand a long time before I can move him to where our friend, Rosemary, is sitting on the couch in its new location. She quickly assesses my situation with Jake, rigid as a steel bar.

"Want me to sit with Jake?"

He's too frozen to acknowledge her but I'm grateful. Seating him is like felling a tree: he goes down rigid, legs sticking out, face pallid as Betty's in the hospital. He's on the edge of meltdown, and I'm skeptical about leaving him. "Can you sit with Rosemary awhile?"

He's too tight to agree or disagree. Cautiously, I move away, greeting old friends and colleagues from the college. Some are accompanied by middle-aged children or, in one case, a grandson Jake's age. The only person I don't recognize is introduced as Betty's oncologist, a quiet, shy woman. Can your oncologist love you more than an estranged son? It's the sort of question Betty would have asked. The answer, apparently, is yes.

Someone says, "She looks so happy." It's the framed photograph we'd brought of the white couch. Betty's head is on Jake's shoulder, a book between them, and they are both laughing.

The college's founder, a tall and tremulous man, retired twenty years, recalls when his daughter was in my writing class thirty years ago. He has similar recollections for the art teacher—ex-truck driver and Korea vet—who recently survived a heart attack, and the pugnacious poet from the mean streets of New York with severe sleep apnea, and the man with a triple bypass who came to teaching from the ministry.

On the couch, Jake's body is at war with itself, doing involuntary isometrics and burning more calories than he will take in this day. Rosemary, leaning close, has managed to bring some light to his face, and I'm thinking we might make it through the service.

Until it begins.

Betty's oldest friend, herself a recent widow of the department and a person Jake knows, starts talking about Betty. A hush falls. And then it comes: a grunt, a shriek of despair. I know from experience it will only escalate and I need to move fast, or else, sweating and screaming, Jake will be impossible to move on foot, and I'll have to drag him out. I can imagine my friends trying to help and not knowing how.

"Do you want to leave?" I whisper.

I know the answer, but he's already surprised me by coming here, and I want to be sure. He expels a desperate *yes*, mouth gaping like one of the mummies on this year's field trip to the Egyptian Museum. *Yes. Please, yes.*

Mourners watch while I stand his rigid body from the couch, whisper thanks to Rosemary, and frog-march him toward the front door. Rosemary waves, but he's oblivious. He has only one thing in mind—exiting to air, light, space. And truth be told, I'm not sorry to miss my own tearful tribute to Betty. At her husband's memorial in this same house, I'd blubbered my concluding remarks: *What would Mel do?*

As the door closes, I hear Betty's best friend, interrupted by our departure, continue where she left off. She's a good public speaker, and her words are measured, loving, and will be, I know, amusing. Any memorial for Betty must be funny.

"I'm really proud of you," I say. "You were great."

Jake is so relieved to be outside that he's into full Buster Keaton mode, taking big looping steps away from Betty's house, her photographs, away from their joy in one another. At the car, I wrap my arms around his waist, raise him into the passenger seat, buckle his seat belt. Her daughter told me that the house will be sold immediately, the house he has memorized, the house where I left them together as I walked Beatrice and threw her tennis ball. She greets us at the car.

I don't tell Jake that we'll never see the house again. Would Mel have concealed that unpleasant fact from him? I have no idea. But in the coming years, whenever Jake seems sad and is asked how he's feeling, he'll type *Betty die*. Followed by *sad*. But he'll never ask to visit her house.

Since many of my former colleagues are his friends, death has become part of our lives. Jake is shocked but accepting. Sometimes I wonder if dying at birth taught him that living and dying are the same. I may know it intellectually, but he's been there.

The Fly and the Elephant

YOU KNOW THE WAY Dad does his ventriloquist act, putting words in my mouth? Well, if you *really* want to know what it's like being a fly on the wall of your own life, let me tell you about our last meeting before my IEP for seventh grade. Mom, Dad, and school people are gathered around a conference table along with my classroom aide and Michelle, my tutor from home. Since they are talking about motivating me, and I do more for Michelle than anybody at school, they are talking to her.

The Speech Language Specialist says, "I've watched her on Dad's home video and it's quite impressive."

Which motivates the Inclusion Specialist to say, "*He's* gotten so much better."

And everyone nods and says *he* certainly is doing better. What else could they say?

"Well, Michelle," the Vice Principal says, "tell us how you motivate *him* (meaning me)."

She says, "I draw a hotel and when Jake gets reward points, he cashes them in by having me fill the rooms with people, trains, African animals, whatever he wants. Other times, we'll read *Alice in Wonderland* on the computer and he'll answer questions."

It's Dad's idea but, for her, I'll do it. She's calm and very beautiful. Call it motivation.

Now Dad's working himself into a lather about this morning's student TV program where I used my talker to announce a clothing drive. The computer speech didn't transmit, so no one heard the announcement, but seventh- and eighth-graders who saw me said, "Jake, that was awesome!"

Which now motivates Dad to tell the Vice Principal: "Why can't he take the video class next year?"

She says, "Sure, we could call it Jake's Corner."

Everyone smiles, not knowing if she's serious.

Meanwhile, in my wheelchair, *he's* thinking: wait a minute, aren't we getting ahead of ourselves here? Isn't there somebody you haven't heard from yet, the fly-on-the-wall? So I deliver a mid-level screech to make my point, motivating a shush from Dad and silence around the table.

The Vice Principal starts slashing at a white board with a colored pen the way teachers do, drawing blocks with arrows, a little like my hotel. She's explaining how complicated my schedule will be next year, and she's talking so fast that Dad slumps. Organization isn't his thing. On the other hand, Mom brightens up because she is very detail-oriented, as a librarian and manager, and quick as lighting about organizational charts.

"Now about electives," the Vice Principal says, "in *his* case we're not talking about Spanish or band."

Since Dad doesn't like dismissive talk about *him*, he snorts: "Whoa, he loves language. Why *not* get him started on a second language?"

Everyone looks at everyone else, and says, "Well, yeah, why not?"

Then Mom says, "He's doing art with Michelle, why not art?"

Thereby motivating the Inclusion Specialist to say that there are great adaptive computer art programs.

Which motivates a paroxysm from Dad: "Yeah, he's getting so good using the mouse with Michelle, why *not* computer art? Or what about composing computer music?"

And everyone is going "Yeah, why not?"

Unlike Mom, Dad is tone deaf and bone ignorant about music,

but people are saying, "Well, yeah. That's true. Music. Why not?"

And now it's time for *him* to intervene, so I deliver a proper screech. You can see their eyes widen like there really *is* an elephant in the room. You can read their minds: We're talking mainstream classes for a kid who screeches? Shouldn't he be in Special Ed?

You've seen *them* getting off that dingy little bus driven by a tough-looking woman. If you were a fly on the wall, you would probably hear the parents of regular students complaining about all the money spent on *them*. What are *they* doing at an elite school like this, with some of the best test scores in the state? Aren't there special programs for *them*? Elsewhere?

Now they're looking at me like a real elephant (my favorite animal), and the Vice-Principal, having just heard what her teachers are complaining about, says, "What if, for example, just as a possible scenario … what if *he* were in Special Ed for a couple of hours a day? Mightn't there be an advantage? *He* could stay in one place, since that works so well at home with Michelle, and *he* could sit in his saddle chair that Dad has talked about so much."

Which is an understatement. Dad won't shut up about the saddle chair and now launches into one of his rants: "Getting him out of that wheelchair," (at least he doesn't say goddamn wheelchair) "that would cripple anybody, is so important. He can use his body a lot more than people think, and the saddle chair gives him better posture, salvages his hips, puts weight on his feet, and gives him the ability to shift around."

Of course the reason we aren't using the saddle chair at school is because it's too difficult to move from class to class. So a Special Ed classroom would be perfect. Thanks, Dad.

And people are going, "Yeah, that's right."

Which means it's time for my very special scream, the one that penetrates eardrums like a sharp pencil, and gets the elephant charging around the room. You can see them thinking: Uh-oh.

"Let us finish here, Jake, we're almost done," Dad says.

Which is about enough for me. Rearing back in my wheelchair, I raise it an octave. Dad, who has no idea what an octave is, leans forward, very dad-like and firm in public, and remonstrates: "That's enough Jake."

You never know how serious he is when he remonstrates. He'd drag me home from Las Lomas swearing at the goddamned teacher, the goddamned principal, and all these fucking state-mandated tests, and then punish *me* for being disruptive. Eventually, he did apologize, but he can be a load.

No one knows what to do with a fly that just became an elephant. The Vice-Principal, whose main job is kicking ass, develops a deep frown that I've seen when I'm wheeled into her office. After a year's experience, my aide sees trouble coming, grabs my chair and wheels me into the courtyard.

"That's no way to behave when people are trying to help you, Jake," he says.

As if I didn't know.

Pretty soon the rest emerge, glad to get outside. They are saying things like, "Good meeting, and thanks for arranging it, and see you at the real IEP meeting in April." (That's when my seventh-grade program is set in legal concrete.) Michelle leaves quietly.

Once they're all gone except Dad and Mom, she says to him, "You know ... Special Ed for a few hours might be a good idea. It would get Jake out of his wheelchair."

Of course, Dad's stupid rant about the wheelchair has got him cornered, and he's pissed, as he frequently is with Mom. Disagreement is our family gestalt. He grumbles: "Maybe. We'll see."

Meaning no way.

With more trouble coming, my aide wheels me toward class, and the last I see of Mom and Dad, they're stiff as boards and talking *at* one another as usual: Spanish? Video? Music? Art? Special Ed?

Who cares? I'll find out soon enough. And the truth is I'd be fine in Special Ed.

As my aide pushes me toward class, we're both wondering what it's going to be—fly, elephant, or actual student? Frankly, none of the above. I'm worn out. I think I'll slump till lunch.

Going to See the Man

AND THEN THERE'S THE QUESTION of surgery hanging over so many kids like Jake with bodies incapacitated by brain damage, bodies twisting or rigid, floppy or frozen in contracture. Some speak, some walk (sort of), some feed themselves, some are continent. Some sit. Some die early. There is no cure for these kids, only hope and melioration mixed with ongoing anxiety.

Jake, nearly immune to colds and flu and with boundless energy and contagious good cheer, is amazingly healthy. He has no permanent contractures (yet), and all his limbs still work (sort of). He can do directed walking, pedal a bike (but not steer). He can, clumsily, use his hands for typing (to my amazement and the surprise of many). He can sit in a chair with support. There is much he can do. Still, at age six, surgery was recommended by his pediatric orthopedist.

It seemed Jake's femurs were coming out of poorly developing sockets (a common issue for kids with high muscle tone and lack of normal weight-bearing), and an osteotomy was required. Femurs would be cut and realigned in his sockets, requiring metal plates, screws, and a body cast for six weeks. Rehabilitation would take many months.

Since a respected surgeon at a respected hospital had told us what was required—case closed.

Almost.

Jake's pediatrician showed us the surgeon's note, which said that

Jacob's parents had missed a regular appointment. Now surgery was urgent, and by implication, we were at fault. I tried to reach him, but an orthopedic surgeon at a famous hospital is not easy to reach. When he did call back, I was driving Jake home from physical therapy. Shaking with anger, I said, "We did not miss that visit. Your letter accusing us of doing so needs to be rewritten."

Perhaps, for legal reasons, surgeons cannot apologize. Perhaps it was only a minor bit of misinformation, no apology was necessary. Perhaps one of his residents wrote the letter. Mistakes happen. Whatever the case, it was clear to me that Jake was only a cipher at the same hospital where birth had almost killed him.

We pushed for second and third opinions from other respected surgeons who, generally, supported the first. That should have settled the issue. Further opposition wasn't Mom's style, but I was in full anger mode. One of Jake's former therapists heard my lament. Perhaps she knew more about this surgeon than she could, professionally, admit. In any case, she gave me the name of a woman who had moved back east and found an exceptional surgeon there.

When I spoke to her, the woman told me that her son had been operated on by the same man who had so angered me and, if possible, she was even angrier. She was driving her son four hours to New Jersey to see a surgeon using innovative techniques on bodies twisted by high muscle tone and short-circuited nerves. "By avoiding crippling surgeries and keeping kids outside casts and hospitals, he preserves childhood. Send him a video of your son."

I did. His email response, including individual frames taken from my video and accompanied by detailed commentary, was more informative than anything we'd heard from local surgeons who had seen Jake in person. This man did not think an osteotomy, requiring a body cast and long recovery, was necessary. And so it came to pass that, after more phone calls and emails, we found ourselves kneeling beside an emergency exit at thirty thousand feet as a flight attendant held up a blanket to screen us changing the diaper of our six-year-old son.

"A touch of cerebral palsy?" she asked delicately.

"Just a touch," I said, still unable to admit it was more than a touch.

A cold draft seeped in beneath the exit door, a draft reaching all the way back to his birth. I imagined the door opening. I imagined being sucked out with Jake in my arms. Would he squeal with delight, as he did pitching off the bed into my arms? Would a surgeon in New Jersey catch him?

During the flight, his mother managed to calm him against the paroxysms of screaming we both feared. Those neurological storms had driven us from many crowded spaces. Like this plane.

In Newark, we pushed him through the airport to a rental car, to a bed and breakfast near the hospital, and next day to the doctor, who bore no resemblance to any surgeon we had seen. He sat with us like a family friend, playing with Jake on a padded bench.

"Look at that," he said.

We looked. Jake lay flat on his back, as usual.

"If he can lie that way, operating on his psoas is not an issue."

It seemed impossible that such a casual observation could eliminate prescribed surgery on a muscle deep in the pelvis. He said, "I treat the patient, not the x-ray."

That response has stuck with me all these years, a philosophy exemplified in surgery the next day. Until he could feel Jake's body going under anesthesia (one of his innovations), he couldn't say exactly what he would do. He would operate through small incisions using the tools of an eye-surgeon (an innovation). Not knowing what might happen, and filled with dread, we waited through surgery for his call and then to see Jake in recovery, pallid in early consciousness, while his surgeon explained what he had done. After some consideration, he'd left the right hip alone and extended the socket of the left hip using bone matrix. He had also administered an alcohol nerve block to relieve the high muscle tone in Jake's legs, which was forcing his hips out of their sockets in the first place. These minimally invasive techniques, we would soon discover, were unheard of on the west coast.

At our exit interview his team talked and joked with us like old friends. The orthotist explained Jake's flexible brace that he'd designed and built on very short notice, a brace that would be admired at home. The neurologist talked about possible ancillary improvement in the upper body. The physical therapist talked about ways for Jake to sit and move. The surgeon himself talked about the particular challenges of Jake's surgery and how he'd addressed them. For the first time, we were experiencing a medical team who had worked together for years, whose experience and respect for one another were now helping us plan Jake's future.

"Forget your expectations," we were told. "Let Jake discover his limits."

He began directed walking a week after our return (unthinkable after an osteotomy). Assisted by his therapist and wearing his admirable brace, he began bashing bolsters and screaming with enthusiasm. He began riding a trike. He began using a keyboard. Might that have been an ancillary improvement of the upper body as suggested by the neurologist? We'll never know. But years later his hips are fine.

I now wonder if Jake was the only one operated on that spring of 1999. Three months later our marriage ended and Jake, in addition to his two functional hips, now had two functional parents in place of one dysfunctional family.

Nine years later we made another trip to New Jersey. Jake's feet were severely pronating, rolling onto his arch while his toes pointed outward. A local surgeon said there was no option to complex surgery, triple arthrodesis, in which his foot would essentially be taken apart and reassembled into something more like a rigid orthotic than a flexible foot. Rehabilitation would be long, complications common and possibly severe. The resulting foot, however, would look good in an x-ray. Even as he explained the operation to us, the local doctor knew we would go back to

New Jersey.

But this time we had to leave behind a dog. My first wife, recently retired as a special education teacher, had become a close friend of our whole family. Carol loved Beatrice and offered to dog sit. She also drove us to the airport for a flight slightly less traumatic than the first because this time we knew the surgeon, and Jake wouldn't need a hospital stay.

Once again, it was Jake, rather than his x-ray, that underwent surgery. Arthroscopic releases eased the overly tight muscles and tendons that were causing his feet to distort, ankle-high casts were applied, and a day after the surgery, we returned home. A month later an orthotist in Marin removed casts from feet that weren't perfect, but were functional, and have remained so to this day.

I often think of a popular analogy from chaos theory: how under the right circumstances, the wings of a butterfly can affect weather in a far-off land. When I slide Jake's foot into a shoe, stand him up, walk with him, I sometimes remember that first surgeon's note, which—like the wings of a butterfly in a far-off country—changed our weather.

Hello, World, Jake Calling

THE PHONE RINGS on my evening walk, and I'm surprised to see who's calling. "Hello," I say, "is this Jake?" knowing full well it is.

Silence.

When excited, he has trouble typing on his talker that serves as a rudimentary cell phone, so I continue uphill toward The Dish, a radio telescope that gives this walk its name.

Finally a deep, middle-aged, male voice says: "This is Jake Wilkins." It's a programmed message delivered at a single keystroke, and this surrogate voice makes me smile.

"Hello, Jake Wilkins," I say.

"What are you doing?" the programmed voice asks.

"What I'm doing is walking the Dish along that path you drove your power chair that time and remembering the time we rode across the Golden Gate Bridge with Beatrice." I don't mention me looking cautiously over the suicide railing, or how skittish Beatrice was about wind and traffic.

I hear Jake typing a word (he prefers spelling to programmed responses), letter by letter, until his touch will cause whatever he's typed to speak over my cell phone.

"Bill," the man's voice says.

I look over Interstate 280 toward Bill's house, hidden by trees in a development where I once mowed lawns at Jake's age.

"I'm looking toward Bill's house right now," I say.

Some professorial types pass (the university is just below me) and look at me talking on the phone. It's the *look*. I want to say: "I don't like it either, people talking on phones. But it's my son. He can't speak."

After a long silence—he may be too excited to type—I decide to help out: "I have a question for you, do you want to hear it?"

Although a preprogrammed *yes* would have been faster, I hear him spelling *y-e-s*.

"What do you want to do on Sunday? Want to swim at Bill's and get a hint?"

He plays a game with Bill that involves guessing the next animal on one of two animal calendars: North American and African. Bill is the only other person he calls regularly, and they talk as we're doing now. Calendars are an obsession of Jake's, and Bill, a man nine years my senior, is indulgent. His hints are fun and educational. Once, when Jake couldn't guess an African animal beginning with *C*, Bill gave us as an additional hint: *plagiarism*. Neither of us could figure that out until Jake's mom, who loves word games, got it right away: *cheetah*.

One day Bill pointed at his shoe to hint at the *Shoe Bill Pelican*. Another animal's name sounded like the Spanish for milk (Jake took Spanish in seventh grade). It was an African antelope indigenous to wetlands, a *Lechwe*. Jake loves these animal calendars, and now he loves his surrogate grandpa with the warm pool, who so late in life has come to love a child, who may be the first he has known from infancy.

Since he already has *yes* typed on the screen, it's easy to say *yes*, he wants to visit Bill on Sunday.

"Okay," I say, "we'll go swimming Sunday and look at calendars. Want to see anything in particular?"

"Lion" is immediate. Frequently used words appear first in his dictionary, so I can guess what's coming, a list of favorite animals. Sure enough: "Moose ... Pelican ... Elk."

Then a glitch. "*H* ..." Silence.

I wait.

Finally *hippopotamus* lumbers over the half mile separating me from our house. Because the computer's enunciation is often unclear, further muddled by wind, I can't make out the next animal.

Jake repeats it three times before I get it: *Lechwe*, our milky friend. I laugh at the computer's pronunciation and suspect he's laughing, too. Next comes "Bull" our shorthand for the *African Cape Buffalo Bull*.

When I say the full name and ask if that's what he means, he types *y*, rather than spell *yes*. He's excited and talking fast now.

Next comes "Duck," the *White-Faced Whistling Duck* we found amusing.

He has a phenomenal memory for these calendars, and I know he wants to continue the list, but San Francisco's fog is rushing toward me, smothering sunset and bringing a cold wind. Chilled in tee shirt and shorts, I interrupt the list.

"Anything on your mind besides more animals?"

Silence.

Fog pours over hills where I once carried Jake in a backpack, covers roads where I pulled him behind my bike or we drove, windows down, on hot summer nights listening to Johnny Cash. He's silent and I feel bad about interrupting his list.

From the crest of the hill, I can see Berkeley where his mom graduated five years before his birth. I can see Silicon Valley transforming his life with email, Facebook, this very phone, and whatever else is coming toward us, too fast to imagine. I can see the hospital where he was born and nearly died, the shopping center where he learned to drive his power chair, where he sat at a café with other families of the disabled from the Bridge School.

Finally, to ease my guilt, I venture a question: "What did you and your tutor have for dinner?"

The response is immediate: "Lasagna."

"What about tomorrow? Shall we ride to a different café for a change?"

"No."

I'm surprised, and to my guilty ear, the surrogate voice sounds reproachful. But at least he's talking again.

"What are we doing Saturday?" I ask.

"*SCZ*" he types, shorthand for Santa Cruz.

"What time should we leave?"

"Eleven."

Then what?

"*BK*"—i.e. Burger King.

"Anything else?" I ask.

He types what sounds like *kiff*. I ask him to repeat several times before I get it: "Oh, Jake, I get it: *Kiss, kiss*."

He often makes loud kisses as a way to show love and gratitude, but since the smacking sounds won't transmit, he's spelled his kiss for the first time ever. I return juicy kissing sounds but find it difficult to pucker, because I'm choked up.

"Kiss," he says again.

I pucker up again.

Then he hits a programmed response: "Goodbye."

"Goodbye, Jake, it was so good talking to you."

Descending into cold dusk, I want to call proudly to passersby: "That was my son. He can't talk."

All over the Bay Area lights are coming on. Beatrice will greet me at the door, follow me to the kitchen where Jake, happy to see me, happy with his phone call, will look up. Likely, he'll rear back in his saddle chair, grinning. His tutor will look pleased. And she should. What he's doing now—talking on the phone, sending text messages or email, using Facebook—has come from her and fellow graduate students I've employed.

Next year another tutor will help him write a keynote speech for the Bridge School graduation. At his own graduation nine years ago, he was unable to endure the ceremony and screamed for release. If he had to sit in front of graduates in wheelchairs and all their well-wishers, he would never agree to a keynote speech. But next year's tutor will help him write in Power Point. That way he can deliver his speech from a safe distance.

In fact, he'll watch through open patio doors behind his audience while they read his words onscreen and hear his opening line: "After this, your life will change."

But that's next year.

Trust

IT'S LIKE A HORROR MOVIE. Something's in the cellar. You know you shouldn't go down there, but unless you do, no horror. And no horror, no movie. My chest is tight, eyes flicking side to side, and I want to take my blood pressure, no doubt soaring into stroke territory.

The *horror* is a law firm's questionnaire that I must complete before my appointment tomorrow. It's about Jake's life after my death. The lead article in this morning's *New York Times* says the first hour is crucial, what cardiologists call the golden hour for a myocardial infarction. The problem is, people ignore symptoms, like a feeling of anxiety or impending doom. Like now. Or discomfort in the chest. Like now. Shortness of breath? Yes. Arrhythmia? Yup.

The monster in the cellar cackles. *An infarction is way too easy for you, Bub. For you it's cancer, dementia, Alzheimer's, or a stroke. Then you can sit in a wheelchair beside your son. No infarction for you.*

I decide to die in my sleep fifteen years from now, and the cellar monster howls with laughter. *You think a man shrunk below six feet with those scrawny white legs, haunted eyes and hesitant steps of the aged will still be living alone with his disabled son fifteen years from now, at eighty-seven? Get real. Die today!*

Okay, then, I'm dead. The man who kept his son out of wheelchairs and on his feet, physically active and free of restraints, the man who found and dismissed therapists, surgeons and schools, who provided financial support and hired tutors … that man is dead. He picks up a pencil and reads the first question: *Specify underlying disability.*

No problem: Cerebral palsy, cannot talk or walk unassisted but cognitively acute (well, maybe a couple of problems in the cognitive area, but no one's been able to figure out just what).

List public assistance available to beneficiary.

Public assistance, of course, is the reason for a Special Needs Trust. Jake will need to be a pauper to keep public assistance: Medi-Cal, In Home Supportive Services, California Children's Services, Golden Gate Regional Center, SSI (after he's eighteen), and half of my Social Security earned as soda jerk, mail carrier, fire fighter, computer operator, crab fisherman, writer. As a teacher I didn't pay into Social Security, so my benefit is a minimal pittance, and Jake receives half-a-pittance. Still, in the topsy-turvy world of special needs, half-a-pittance could threaten his future.

Granted, I do wonder whether a boy with a house to live in (unless my final days require a reverse mortgage) really needs public assistance. However, advice on this subject has been unanimous. You need a Special Needs Trust.

Which of the following are acceptable or unacceptable? Living in private residence? Group home? Public care facility? Public institution?

That's easy! I've spent years jackhammering away stone steps, building 2000 feet of deck, tearing out walls, widening doors, to make this house accessible. No group homes, facilities, institutions for my son. No way. He will live here.

What sort of activities do you wish to encourage the beneficiary to participate in: Special Olympics? Sporting activities? Sporting events? Cultural activities? Religious activities? All of the above?

Well, he didn't much care for Special Olympics, and he freaked out at the Giants' game, but never mind. Cultural activities, of course, and religious activities? Well, the dead man had no fondness for organized religion, but why not? *All of the above.*

Do you want beneficiary to maintain contact with Grantor's family?

That poses a problem since beneficiary *is* the Grantor's only immediate family. I guess he could maintain contact with himself. And his mom has lots of family, so, yes, *maintain contact.*

If yes, what family expenditures are appropriate: Purchase gifts to acknowledge events such as birthdays, holidays, etc? Pay for beneficiary to travel to family events? Pay for family members to visit beneficiary?

Whatever. *All of the above.*

List possible members of an Advisory Committee for your Special Needs Trust, persons you trust and whom you believe can assist with appropriate personal care for the beneficiary and assist in the financial decision making, and indicate their strengths and weaknesses.

Uh-oh. Jake's mother is eighteen years younger than the dead man, and though they sometimes disagree about their son's direction, her love for Jake is absolute. After the deceased's untimely death at ninety-two (I've decided to give myself twenty years), Jake's mom will, of course, be on the committee. As will Carol, the dead man's first wife, assuming she outlives him. But who else?

Well, now that I'm living another twenty years, my unadopted step-daughter will be 73, the same age as Jake's mom. And aging friends? Forget it. The cellar monster is howling with delight because this is what he's been looking forward to, that exquisite moment when a torture victim will say anything to stop the torture. I begin giving names and qualities of anyone I can think of: this person lacks promptness but is a financial wizard, this one's flighty but with an iron will, dreamy but insightful, indecisive but loving, spewing out whatever will shut up the monster. I can fix it later.

Sure, the monster says, *with you it's always later. Only this time you just ran out of later, and still you can't face it.*

True. But then I'm saved by the next question: *Would you like the trust to terminate and distribute the assets to the beneficiary if beneficiary is no longer dependent on public benefits and has been gainfully employed for a stated period of time.*

You mean beneficiary could become an heir? *If?* If what? He's becoming more literate and independent, medical science and technology are exploding, so why not gainful employment? Someday. The possibility lifts me out of stroke territory, and I impale the monster:

Yes.

If yes, how long should beneficiary be gainfully employed before termination?

Who cares? If he's gainfully employed, let's terminate. How about two years?

If beneficiary is clean and sober for specific period of time?

He's got no choice.

If beneficiary is compliant with his or her psychiatric treatment?

Are you kidding?

Should trustee require a drug test to demonstrate compliance?

No.

How is property to be distributed upon death of beneficiary? To beneficiary's descendants?

His descendants? True, he's got pubic hair and boners, the usual precursors to descendants, but actual descendants? As a sperm donor? Or wait a minute, I seem to recall a woman on top requires nothing but a boner, which he can certainly provide. And the view is splendid. He's a good-looking kid with assets. Why not descendants? I'm starting to like this.

I stab the monster again. *Yes.*

Distribute to beneficiary's spouse? Well, some wheelchair-bound men seem conjugally content. So why not? Why the fuck not? Stab.

Distribute to trust maker's descendants?

My sole descendant just died, so who cares? Sure. Stab.

Please write a Memorandum of Intent directing your Advisory Committee as to your wishes for the beneficiary.

Wishes? Jake will be living in this house. True, I never wanted to live here myself and escaped with friends, girlfriends, wives, for fifty years of travel and teaching. How could *he* escape?

And just that fast I'm careening toward an abyss I have not wanted to look into. Could this, my clearest wish for him, to live in this house, be too restrictive? Lonely? Might a group home—an idea I detest but his mother doesn't—provide companionship and escape? Might she be right? The monster grunts.

The dead man is sitting in what could pass for a farmhouse: scarred wooden floors, east-facing casement windows, a huge plank table. Morning light spills over whitewashed walls, pale blue counter tops, and pans hanging on the wall. His son has sat at this table for sixteen years, six years with his mother and father, then with his father, caregivers and tutors.

The dead man's pulse is off the chart, carotids writhing, breathing shallow. It's Sunday afternoon, and he needs to pick up his son at Mom's house.

Dear Committee Members:

Why don't you accompany us down the wheelchair ramp from Mom's house? Open the passenger door of the Honda Element. Say to Jake: "Give me a straight body." When he stands straight, wrap your arms around his thighs and lift him, the way athletes celebrate victory by raising one another in their arms. Lower his heels onto the running board, let him bend his legs and lower his butt onto the passenger seat.

Say, "Give me soft legs," and he'll do his best to relax the muscles that let him stand and walk in the first place. Swing his feet under the dash, strap him in, and let Beatrice jump into the backseat through that odd rear door on the Element known as a suicide door.

Now here's the tricky part. As you drive off, you'll need to be thinking in tandem and that requires frequent eye contact, not the safest way to drive, but you'll get the hang of his enthusiastic yesses versus half-hearted yesses, full body nos versus uncertainties that might go either way and give you leverage. Offer choices and look for the response. Where for a bike ride? What time to visit Bill? What's for dinner? If he gestures at the bag of chips he likes to eat while riding in the car, pull one out, glance over for an open mouth and then, feeling his lips against your fingers, deliver the chip. It's like feeding a baby bird. He'll crunch and swallow, and just that fast you're intimate in a way not common between fathers and adolescent sons.

And that's just five minutes of a day walking together, standing together, getting on and off the bike together, eating together, changing diapers together, swimming together—a day of constant physicality, glance, intuition, communication and love. Now you know what I want for my son after my death.

Epilogue

YOU MAY HAVE SEEN HIM at Menlo Atherton High School (his father's alma mater) driving his power chair down crowded corridors with Beatrice on one side, his aide on the other. You may have seen her, an assistance dog not to be touched by strangers, being surreptitiously petted by students. You may have seen his teacher, who welcomed her presence in class, taking her for walks.

You might have seen her at a café famous for entrepreneurs and venture capitalists, Stanford students and tech wizards. She would have been lying patiently beside his bike while her master drank fresh orange juice through a straw held to his lips by his father. They are so well known here they have become invisible. You may have seen them at other cafés in Palo Alto, Menlo Park, Redwood City, Mountain View, Santa Cruz, or at reunions with children and parents from the Bridge School at a Mexican restaurant near Stanford.

Perhaps, three abreast, they came toward you on a sidewalk, and you allowed them to pass with none of the resentment you might have felt for three high school boys. You may even have stopped to praise the beautiful Beatrice, so sweet, her face so open to joy, not unlike the young man on his bike. Perhaps you saw them parked inside the door at Trader Joes and crouched to talk to him, while illicitly petting Beatrice.

Family calendars from 2000 to 2012 show him riding through sagebrush on Monitor Pass, through the meadow near their cabin, or in back of a ski boat laughing into the wind with Beatrice, or on the far side of Sonora Pass beside the Walker River, Jake in his EZ Rider wheelchair, Beatrice alert and wet beside him, Dad kneeling behind them.

You might even have encountered them on the trail, this odd group coming toward you, or been sitting in the hot springs as Jake floated past in his life vest and Beatrice kept her eye on him. At Bill's pool (until she was discouraged from doing so) she would leap in to save Jake from drowning in his life vest. She'd grab hold of the vest, drag him to the steps, and then try to pull him up to safety. Now she knows better, but this isn't Bill's pool, and she's worried.

Photos show her emerging from the surf at Ocean Beach in San Francisco, while Master Jake is off seeing his physical therapist. And sleeping on the bed with her master, at a proper remove, since even a dog devoted to his welfare, who would tow him out of swimming pools and pull his bike, a working dog, had to keep her distance because, once upon a far-off time, a hissing cat had made him wary of animals.

She's there in photos of barbecues on Dad's back deck with Jake's mom and many of the people who helped him through the years: caregivers, tutors, teachers, counselors, friends. There's even a video of Jake driving his very first power wheelchair, steering with his head as Dad followed with his video camera—people dodging out of the way, and Beatrice, confused by sudden turns, getting tangled in her leash.

Fortunately, no photos exist of that time at Burger King in Sonora when Beatrice, lying on the lawn in front of the car and out of sight, was left behind. I drove back fearing she might have followed the car onto the highway and been killed, yelling at the top of my voice, *I can't believe it. I can't believe I did that*, Jake laughing at my panic. She lay peacefully on the grassy knoll at Burger King, well-trained and dutiful beyond imagining.

Dog parks were a little gross for her refined nature. Around cantankerous and hyper dogs, she, like her master, was cautious. Oh, she might indulge in a discreet sniff fest, offer a crouching invitation to play, even engage in a brief communal run, but more often she was solitary. Like her master (and his father), crowds were not her thing.

There are no photographs of meals at home and that's just as well because they were pretty gross. Food leaked off bibs, lap, wheelchair—juicy strands of spaghetti, bits of garlic bread, salad, ice cream, fig bars, yogurt—onto the floor where Beatrice did her best to ignore it. As time passed, she began patrolling our perimeter until, finally, she could lie with her head between her master's feet, waiting for manna. What her ancestors must have done at bloody medieval feasts. The hardwood floors gleamed.

For years she stayed home from school because protocol required an aide have the same training Jake's parents had, and that was beyond impractical. So when Jake was at school, Beatrice stayed home. But Frank, his new aide at high school, became a big brother leading Jake through the intricacies and hazards of adolescence, and his ease with Beatrice was quickly apparent. Soon she was going to school and there, at last, she found her rightful place in Jake's world.

As the only dog legally allowed at Menlo Atherton High, she was the assistance animal she had always aspired to be: loved by classmates, by his teacher who appreciated her calming effect on students with disabilities, by the adaptive PE teacher who incorporated her in games, giving her foot pads to wear on the hardwood floors as she nosed the ball toward Jake. Beatrice, Jake and Frank were widely known around school, well-liked, cheerfully greeted in crowded corridors.

There is, however, one final photograph that needs to be mentioned. It's on the fireplace mantle and shows Jake sitting in front of bleachers, classmates seated behind him. He's looking away from the camera while Beatrice, beside him, stares toward us, tongue out as if panting on a hot day. But it's not the weather. It's cancer. The photo was taken on an April Friday when it still seemed possible that medication might halt the disease.

The following Monday, swollen and unable to stand, Beatrice lies stretched across the rear floor of the Honda. We wait for the vet to appear with all the car doors open: Jake beside me in the passenger seat, his mom on the floor in back holding Beatrice's head, and next to her at the rear door, Carol, who has driven across California to be here with the dog who helped bring us all together.

I had learned that our vet was the brother of my roommate at Reed College, the only other student from Menlo Atherton High, a man who had died years before. But his brother has become more than a vet to Beatrice. He is a friend to all of us, and as he approaches the car, sixty years of my life converge in the back of a Honda Element.

He injects Beatrice with a tranquilizer and she relaxes, well-loved and unconscious, before the final lethal injection. Then, on a stretcher, she is carried away from three crying adults.

And one more adult, Jake, now eighteen, sits silent in the front seat, feelings masked and unknown to the rest of us, who are sobbing and trying to comfort one another. Such strange vessels we are, carrying our cargo of experience. He carries his in silence. These days when something is bothering him, he will type *sad Bea* and look to his mom or me to explain what that might mean to a stranger. But what do we know?

His actions must speak for him. He's less fearful around dogs, will reach out to touch them, is even inclined to have another dog. Let that suffice for language.

Under the guidance of their remarkable teacher, Jake's class created a garden on some unused land between buildings. The paths (wide enough for a wheelchair) are paved with tiles made by students, some with their names, some not. *Jake* and *Beatrice* appear on separate tiles. Mrs. Price and her students, along with Frank and other aides, hauled topsoil and gravel, shaped miniature hillocks, laid tiles, and planted flowers. Jake contributed a solar fountain, and the reclaimed space was christened the Garden of Memory and Imagination. Though the area is small, the paths meander in a way that might have pleased Alice in Wonderland, strolling with kings, queens, and mythical beasts. Sunflowers tower, Mexican sage and Peruvian lilies draw bees and hummingbirds, and the garden draws students. Some sit on a bench with a bronze plaque: *Beatrice, Canine Companion, 2000–2011.*

So, this school I left as a teenager, resisting my own education and toting psychic baggage, Jake will leave as a twenty-two-year-old man. A man who has learned a measure of independence and community, a man becoming increasingly literate and functional.

I left behind my picture in a yearbook.

Our son will leave a Garden of Memory and Imagination.

Acknowledgments

Without Joe Stroud and Rachel Harris there would be no book. Joe's long faith and friendship kept me going, and Rachel's astonishing ability to see connections and edit the whole work brought it into being.

There have been many partisans in Jake's life who have helped us along the way. Some are named in this book while others appear anonymously: Bill Wiegand, Carol Hoge, Regina DeCosse, Lama Tharchin Rinpoche, Shane Jackson, Janet Babb, Joe Stroud, Dick and Sue Lundquist, Dan and Alice Harper, Mel and Betty Tuohey, Linda Kitz, Rosemary Brogan, Robley Levy, Andrew Vahldieck, Peggy Simon, Gayle Piper, John Allen, Dr. Roy Nuzzo and his superb team in New Jersey, the "bike guys" Ranier Zaechelein and Rich Shing at Menlo Velo and Dave Plymouth at Abilities First Cycle in Redding, and of course, Canine Companions, Beatrice, and her wonderful vet, Dave Roos.

Teachers, specialists, and aides at a series of schools have made enormous contributions to Jake's education and development. Support from the Bridge School has been invaluable from the start, with Aileen Arai, Sarah Baroody, Elisa Kingsbury, Kelly Rinehart, Chris Toomey, Tike De Marco, and Michelle Bishop having been particularly helpful. We will always be grateful to Nancy Hendry and the teachers and staff at Laurel school; to Charlene Mattos, Martha Rosenthal, Kristin Ocon, Lois Nissman, and Evelyn Lorton at Encinal School; to Michael Moore, Susan Churba, Diane Glasser, and Tony Martin at Hillview Middle School; and to Susan Price, Jim Bell, Mark Leeper, Betsy Snow, Gayle Oytas, Frank Cornejo and many others at Menlo Atherton High School. Our gratitude also goes out to all of Jake's caregivers and tutors over the years: Sonam Thunden, Michelle Brown, Jennifer Hansen, Michelle Kharrazi, Christine Velez, Ayelet Arbuckle, Alicia Wall, and Katie Knarr—and to Linzy Branson, Junior Brandao, and Frank Cornejo, who remain an indispensable part of Jake's life. And what would our lives have been without Linda Kitz and Diana Heberger, Claire Biancalana and Bill Kelsay, Holt and Margaret Murray, Ellen Stewart and Dave Purdy, Ellen Scott, John Chandler, Donna Mekis and Mort Marcus, Nick and Sue Roberts, Ellen Stuck and Andre Neu, Susan Munsey, Regina DeCosse and Stefan Graves and their son Rowan, Elizabeth Duncan, Werner Schlieper, Elva Vasquez, Chris Wright, and Rick Escobar. And then there are the partisans brought into Jake's world by his mother, Jennifer Wilkins, who has her own stories to tell.

Along the way I've been guided by Jody Gelb, who drew on her experience as a Bridge School parent in reading this work. I have received helpful comments on many of these chapters from my friends John Chandler, Bill Broder, and Dave Walker; from my Santa Cruz writers' group: Jerry Kay, Cathy Warner, Natalie Serber, Margaret Kinstler, Doreen Devorah, Barbara Fuller, Susan Drake, and Chris Mason; from my Menlo Park writers' group: Jim Spencer, Rob Swigart, Nancy and Harold Farmer, and Antoinette May; from Abigail Thomas and her Alta students; from Jan Pendleton, Paul Reasenberg, Kinga Czegeni, Lynette Mullens, Ayelet Arbuckle, and Dave Roos. And in recent years the entire text has been read by Bill Wiegand, Elizabeth Duncan, Joe Stroud, Ellen Scott, Barbara and Ray March, Monica Hersch, Bruce Hobson, and Carol Hoge, who brings so much knowledge, love, and perspective to these stories. Finally, deep appreciation goes to Wendy Madar of Lychgate Press, who read this manuscript and believed in the project.

Kirby Wilkins, a graduate of Stanford and San Francisco State creative writing programs, is the author of a book of short stories, *Vanishing*, and two novels, *King Season* and *Quantum Web*. He taught English and fiction writing at Cabrillo College in Aptos, California, for over 30 years. He has also led writing workshops at the Foothill Writers' Conference and the Surprise Valley Writers' Conference. Since the birth of his son, Jake, in 1992, his writing has moved in unexpected directions. Every day his son reveals more about life and love, and this, it turns out, is the only reason left for him to write.

CPSIA information can be obtained
at www.ICGtesting.com
Printed in the USA
LVHW111322180422
716527LV00015B/89